Books and Prints, Past and Future

Books and Prints, Past and Future

Papers presented at The Grolier Club Centennial Convocation, 26–28 April 1984

The Grolier Club
New York: 1984

THIS BOOK IS MADE POSSIBLE BY A GENEROUS GRANT FROM THE
CARL AND LILY PFORZHEIMER FOUNDATION, INC.

ISBN: 0-910672-02-4

1000 COPIES PRINTED

Contents

GORDON N. RAY
Introduction   *vii*

MARY C. HYDE
Grolier Watching By a Lady, 1943–1966   *1*

G. THOMAS TANSELLE
The Evolving Role of Bibliography, 1884–1984   *15*

ROBERT DARNTON
Scholarship and Readership: New Directions
   in the History of the Book   *33*

ROBERT GIROUX
The Future of the Book   *53*

JAMES THORPE
The Future of the Book   *61*

BENJAMIN M. COMPAINE
An Introduction to the New Literacy   *71*

ANDREW ROBISON
The Museum Curator and Fine Prints: Past, Present, and Future   *89*

WALTER BAREISS
A Print Collector's View   *101*

EBERHARD W. KORNFELD
A Print Dealer's View   *109*

FRANK STELLA
An Artist's View of Prints   *121*

DANIEL BELL
Gutenberg and the Computer: *Disparate de Miedo*
    (The Folly of Fear)   *125*

vi

Introduction

GORDON N. RAY

The Grolier Club, America's oldest association of book and print collectors, marked its centennial with a convocation in New York on 26, 27, and 28 April 1984. The full schedule of proceedings, for which our clubhouse served as the nerve center, was attended by about two hundred members and guests, all that could be accommodated. The papers in this volume, ten delivered during the course of three seminars and the eleventh at the final dinner, will remain the most tangible testimony to the event. Seven of these essays have as their principal theme what the book has meant and what it will mean to those devoted to its welfare. The four discussions of prints were inspired by a similar effort to see that field in historical perspective.

Our program was conceived before the Library of Congress announced its study of 'the Book of the Future,' which was undertaken in response to the feeling, mildly expressed by one senator, that 'perhaps the future of the book is not as solid as it might appear.' Since we did not regard ourselves as 'late arrivals on a stricken field,' no such nagging anxiety inspired our planning. On the whole, the papers as delivered justified our confidence. Neither was it much impaired by the ensuing discussions, which to our regret could not conveniently be reported here. The convocation left us with the conviction that we have been part of a lively age of book collecting, bibliographical study, and book history, and that this age bids fair to continue.

Our first seminar was devoted to retrospective essays. It began with Mary Hyde's 'Grolier Watching By a Lady, 1943–1966,' a timely reminder of the unique role that the Club has played in the American book world. Mrs. Hyde, our vice president and the first woman elected to membership, is one of the premier collectors of her time, as well as an accomplished scholar and writer. There is no more authoritative commentator on bibliography than G. Thomas Tanselle, the Club's secretary and the current president of the Bibliographical Society of America. He, too, is a scholar whose fundamental contributions are based in part on his activities as a collector. We were fortunate in securing Robert C. Darnton, professor of history at Princeton University, as our third speaker. His profound investigations of eighteenth-century French documents, which rival the best work being done in France, have helped to make printing and publishing history the important field of study that it has become today.

Paralleling these historical papers were three addresses on the future prospects of the book. As one of the country's outstanding editors and publishers, Robert Giroux, chairman of the board of Farrar, Straus and Giroux, made sure that we would view this subject in shrewdly realistic terms. James Thorpe, director emeritus of the Henry E. Huntington Library and a former professor of English at Princeton University, brought to his wide-ranging speculations a lifetime of study and experience. Finally, the context of the computer revolution was presented by Benjamin Compaine, executive director of the Program on Information Resources Policy at Harvard University.

These were the first and third seminars. The second took cognizance of the fact that the Grolier, in its origin and again today after a period of neglect, has been a Club of print collectors as well as book collectors. As in the discussions of books, there was a consistent effort by our international panel of experts to see present-day collecting in the frame provided by collecting of the past. So Andrew Robison, curator of prints and drawings at the National Gallery of Art, considered the subject from the museum point of view, our fellow member Walter Bareiss drew on the knowledge accumulated in forty years of intensive collecting, and a well-known dealer,

Eberhard Kornfeld of Bern, offered the perspective acquired through long service in a major auction house. Special distinction was lent to the occasion by the participation of Frank Stella, one of America's leading painters and printmakers, who defined the role of the artist in the 'fine arts' printing of original graphics.

The concluding address by Daniel Bell, Henry Ford II Professor of Social Sciences at Harvard University, is an early report on one aspect of the crowning project of its author's distinguished career, his attempt to provide a schematic framework for the so-called 'information revolution.' Himself an ardent book collector, Mr. Bell could be relied upon to hold the balance even between Gutenberg and the computer.

Books and Prints, Past and Future

Grolier Watching By a Lady, 1943–1966

MARY C. HYDE

The first time I ever heard of The Grolier Club was when Randolph Adams, director of the Clements Library at the University of Michigan, came to dinner with Don and me in Grosse Pointe in 1940, shortly after we were married. We were talking about book collecting and Randy saw the gleam in Don's eye.

When Don said that he had just accepted an offer to join a New York law firm and that we were moving East in a few months, Randy cried out—he was a very enthusiastic man—'You ought to be a member of The Grolier Club. You *have* to be!'

Don said it would be a great honor to belong to such a club, but, as Randy knew, our collection was very small: some first editions of English and American authors, Don's few Johnsons and other eighteenth-century books, and my handful of Elizabethan quartos.

'Quite all right, quite all right,' said Randy, and I looked at him with great interest. 'Now when you get to New York,' he said, 'try to meet some book collectors and go to book auctions. And get to know the booksellers. And I'll be along soon.'

When we arrived in New York we dropped into bookshops whenever there was a free moment, and within a month we attended the Red Cross sale at the Plaza Hotel. There, in the distance, we glimpsed some of the greats of the book world, Belle Greene, Dr. Rosenbach, Arthur Houghton, and Mrs. A. Edward Newton, alas, in widow's black. Soon after this came the promised visit of Randy. He took us at once to lunch at Dr. Rosenbach's house on 51st Street, opposite St. Patrick's Cathedral—a Lucullan and eye-opening experience that went on from one o'clock till five. That same evening we were introduced to Arthur Houghton, and the next week Arthur came to our apartment, looked over the books on our shelves, and made innumerable notes on three by five cards (advice on book collecting). He gave us the cards and promised to introduce William Jackson the next time the Houghton librarian came down from Harvard.

The following month we went to the opening session of the Newton Sale (16 April 1941) with the Houghtons, Dr. Rosenbach, and John Fleming, and during the course of the evening we met Lessing Rosenwald, Frank Hogan, and Lionel Robinson, the London bookseller. We also met William Jackson, and this event was prelude to my Grolier 'watch,' for it was Bill Jackson who first brought Don to 47 East 60th Street, to have tea with Miss Granniss, the redoubtable librarian, who, by this time, had been at the Club for almost forty years. Miss Granniss liked her afternoon tea and book talk and presided over all very graciously, welcoming any member and his friends who cared to drop by—a pleasant custom. This afternoon the door was opened by James Lovett, the loyal Club steward, slow-moving and frank-speaking: 'Well, Mr. Jackson, you got a candidate?'

Don was taken upstairs to Miss Granniss's office (now the print room). He was introduced to George McKay, the Club's curator and also a well-known bibliographer on the side. Don was also introduced to a number of Grolier members. He had a very enjoyable time—particularly with Frederick Adams. I heard a lot about The Grolier Club when Don came home that night. He said he hoped he had enough credentials because he certainly wanted to belong. Apparently, he was more acceptable than he realized, for Fred Adams has told me that 'After the tea party at The Grolier Club, we quickly dragooned Don into becoming a member.' Fred Adams, vice president at the time, proposed Don and Bill Jackson seconded him. I have a note on my engagement calendar for 14 October 1943, 'D and M at Morgan Library. Tom Streeter talk,' and added above this, in big letters, 'DON ELECTED TO GROLIER CLUB!' For over twenty years 'The Grolier Club' appeared on my calendar pages more frequently than anything else. Usually in such phrases as 'D at Grolier, M at work . . . at theatre . . . out for dinner' because, as you remember, most meeting invitations read, 'Guests may be invited, *but not including ladies.*' I did enjoy the Saturday afternoon teas, though, and the Christmas meeting, and one or two other evenings during the year when ladies *were* included.

When Don was elected to the Club, he was in the Navy working on contracts, and though stationed at the time in New York, he was too busy to be active at the Grolier. The Club itself was not a very lively place. In fact, wartime president Harry Peters (1939–42) had viewed the conflict abroad and Roosevelt's policies at home with such alarm that he proposed selling the clubhouse and much of its contents and moving the remains into an apartment. Edwin Bechtel, the president who followed (1943–46), held a more optimistic view of the future and was able to rally enough support from young members to hold off the proposed move, but, still, very little was going on. Miss Granniss retired early in 1944 and the ritual of tea was abandoned. George McKay assumed the title of librarian in addition to that of curator and competently handled both jobs, but he was not at all interested in furthering any social book-gatherings.

The only real activity in the Club was on the part of some of the young men who had held fast with President Bechtel. They were stirring things up by rejuvenating the 'Bowsers,' a group originally formed in the late thirties, to sup and bowse 'from horn and can.' 'The Bowsers organized small dinners, where one brought books to show and discuss,' and they 'met occasionally for drinks. It was not a closed circle—the purpose was to get the members to talk about books, use the library, and enjoy each other's company.' Informality certainly appears to have been the order of the evening, for the 'Bowsers' Log Book' is virtually blank. 'Bowsers for Don 7 P.M.,' I have on my calendar for 13 February 1945, and in his Grolier file is his acceptance: 'It has been much too long,' he wrote, 'since I have gathered with the august body.'

By March of 1946 Don was freed from terminating Navy contracts and now he had time to enjoy The Grolier Club—and to pick up the threads of his law practice. His most fascinating and difficult client was a Grolier member, Ralph Isham, who was trying to sell his Boswell papers.

The Club made no official demands on Don until 1948, when Sinclair Hamilton, as House chairman, asked him to serve on his committee. Right away I began hearing about the redecorating of the stair well and upper halls so they would 'no longer look like a stage set for *Crime and Punishment*.' I also heard all about the celebration for George McKay's twenty-fifth anniversary at the Club; it was also Lovett's twenty-fifth anniversary as steward, and I was riveted to hear that Lovett had made a double celebration for himself by getting married! 'Now,' as Sinclair Hamilton concluded his annual report for 1948, 'there is a couple in charge of the clubhouse.'

Don must have worked effectively on the House Committee because the next year he was made chairman, which title made him a member of the Council. This honor dictated the whole pattern of our lives from then on. It meant that, though we tried to live in the country, Don had a commitment in New York City every second Thursday evening of the month (with the exception, of course, of June, July, and August). Trips for pleasure were planned around Grolier Council dates; business obligations were made compatible whenever possible. 'The meetings of the Council were inviolable on our calendars,' Arthur Houghton has confirmed, 'none of us would have missed one.' He cited an example from the period when Irving Olds was president of the Club (1951–54) and also chairman of U.S. Steel. This giant corporation was facing a strike, scheduled to begin on a second Thursday. 'Would Irving Olds come to conduct the Club Council meeting? Of course, he was there,' said Arthur, 'and the most important item on the agenda—the business which took up most of the evening—was whether the Club's refrigerator should be repaired or whether funds should be appropriated to buy a new machine.'

I asked Arthur whether the Council meetings were sometimes a bit rowdy; I had heard the rumor that they were. Arthur's answer was firm: 'The meetings of the Council were *never* rowdy. Amusing, yes, but never rowdy. We always dressed in black tie. The meetings ran precisely according to Robert's *Rules of Order*. Formality and wit are a great combination.'

I do not know when the custom started, but after Council meetings a group of hardy survivors would adjourn to the Carlton House. There they would sit at a round table, talk things over and listen to Daphne (later Mrs.

Geoffrey Hellman) render popular romantic songs on the harp. Fritz Liebert, I am told, was always 'the first to leave—dashing back to Grand Central Station to catch the midnight milk train to New Haven. Fritz never left before 11:45, sometimes at 11:50, yet he always made the train. The rest of us,' my informant says, 'usually got Don to pay the bill before we drifted away.'

This statement makes me understand for the first time why Don began to suggest to the group that they drop in on Howard Goodhart at the St. Regis, or some other 'hospitable soul' nearby, or come to *our apartment* on 63rd Street (later, the new apartment, on Sutton Place). More and more often, it was our apartment, and I was directed to have nightcap preparations at the ready. Don would telephone just before the group left the Club. I would jump up from a nap, put on a long dress, and get out the ice.

For a few years, our very attractive niece, a Wellesley graduate, was working on an advanced degree in Russian at Columbia. She had literary interests and the ability to hold her own in any discussion, so I would telephone her—say at eleven o'clock—she would hop right into a cab and come down to help. Bibliophiles, I learned at the beginning, were nocturnal creatures. I remember one night when we all stayed up till 4 A.M., arguing about who was best suited to be the next librarian of Congress. And when we finally parted company (without coming to any agreement) no one thought of commenting on the lateness of the hour. Just a happy evening. As Don said, 'No one has more fun in life than book collectors!'

In 1950 the Bowsers metamorphosed into an official committee of the Club—'Special Functions'—a far more dignified title, but with the same goal: a good dinner and good talk. Valla Lada-Mocarski was the first chairman and Don, who had become secretary of the Club, was on his committee. I soon began hearing about the Special Function dinners, which were held in the Council room—as they are now. Twenty members were all Lovett would tolerate (though he was later cajoled into serving thirty). When I asked about the dinners, Don said, 'Two: one menu, steak; other menu, chicken; alternating.' Well-known persons in many fields were asked to speak on subjects of their choice, most often related to books or prints, but not necessarily so. Each member of the Club received at least one invitation a year. 'Oversubscribed again!' Don would report cheerfully when he came home.

We usually invited the speakers Don had persuaded to come to visit us later at the farm, and this was a very pleasant form of 'Grolier watching' for me. We entertained the Foy Kohlers (Foy had been in college with Don and was then a counselor at our embassy in Moscow, later our ambassador and an adviser for the Grolier trip to Russia, which never, alas, took place); Milton Caniff, the cartoonist, who had been art editor for Don's senior yearbook, of which Don had been the editor-in-chief; the Percy Muirs of Elkin Mathews; Frank and Kitty Francis from the British Museum; the Birleys from Eton; and R. W. Chapman, recent secretary of the Oxford Press and renowned Johnsonian. Dr. Chapman was the most eccentric and demanding guest we *ever* had—needed only four hours sleep and required early morning tea at 4:30 A.M. But he *was* a great help in the library.

I enjoyed all these visitors but I enjoyed the Grolier excursions even more. I did not feel at all deprived and unfulfilled. I don't think the other 'wives of members' did either; we had plenty of privileges and absolutely no responsibilities. I felt badly, though, about ladies on their own who were ideally qualified to join the Club except for gender. Way back in 1919 Amy Lowell wanted to be a member, and A. Edward Newton wrote her, 'I damn near broke up the Grolier Club in my effort to have you made a member and I am not through with it yet.' Miss Lowell replied, 'Thank you very much for your efforts on my behalf with the Grolier Club. It is certainly a curse being a woman.' This was before my time, but I did know Belle Greene and Dorothy Miner, to say nothing of a bright array of contemporaries who had the highest qualifications. Among them was a very dear friend, a Vassar classmate, who had her own printing press, and she took a practical approach: 'My *next* husband,' she said, 'is going to be a member of The Grolier Club—so I can go on those trips.'

The trips were wonderful: weekend excursions to Boston (1950), Washington (1953), Philadelphia (1954), Baltimore (1957), Charlottesville (1958), and, in 1959, the unforgettable first excursion abroad—two weeks in England, with a weekend in Paris. This trip was the most spectacular event of the Club's seventy-fifth anniversary. But don't forget the two other important anniversary events: the publication of the superlative *Grolier 75* by Monroe Wheeler's committee and the transformation of the old 'mezzanine lounge' into the beautiful new rare book room, the anniversary gift of the Council members. This room completed the other half of the Bowsers' goal—making it possible for members to show and enjoy each other's books. Alexander Davidson, the new Club librarian (after the retirement of George McKay in 1958), took a special interest in the rare book room, and Bradley Martin commented at a Council meeting, in a purposeful way, 'Yes, it's beautiful, but when's there going to be a show?' Bradley was instantly made the first chairman of the 'Committee on Small Exhibitions.'

President Waller Barrett and the Council were hard at work on all three major anniversary projects through 1958 and early 1959. Don, now vice president, was particularly involved with the excursion abroad, and perhaps it was he who had early on suggested at a Council meeting that London member Lionel Robinson be put in charge of arrangements in England. Anyway, Lionel had demurred by return mail but recommended a travel agency, Ashton Mitchell, and in short order Frank Crome, a seasoned planner of royal visits, was put in charge of the Grolier excursion, in which more than one hundred members (including ladies) were taking part.

Don volunteered to go to London before the official party to help with arrangements. So we departed in early April and worked for a week in the basement of the Ashton Mitchell Agency on Old Bond Street. I remember one day, when we were struggling with a seating chart, Frank asked, 'Are there any members of your Club who do not speak to each other?' Shocked, we assured him that we were all very friendly, but it was nice to know that he took even the impossible into consideration.

On Sunday, 19 April 1959, we, Frank Crome, and Mrs. Teague, his indispensible assistant, met the chartered Grolier Pan Am plane at Heathrow. President Barrett and Cornie came down the ramp, followed by Fred Adams, carrying the banner, 'Ex Libris.' The excited but sleepy travelers were whisked off to their hotels in two huge buses; a third huge bus followed with their luggage. During our two-weeks' trip we never saw our luggage, except in our hotel rooms. Blissful memory!

It was a thrilling trip: London, Oxford, Eton, Cambridge, excursions to great houses and collections in the country, and the long weekend in Paris. Everywhere we were shown overwhelming hospitality, and at almost every stop, so it seemed to me, Bill Scheide saw yet another Gutenberg Bible and Dick Gimbel bought another amusing hat.

My only sizable responsibility on the trip was to organize a 'Theatre Night' for the ladies on the evening when the Club members asked exceedingly distinguished English guests to dine with them at Stationers' Hall. Well, we ladies had a very nice time, and when we were rejoined by the members, *they* were euphoric . . . magnificent banquet, incredible guest list, and a great address by Sir David Eccles, who said that books were his solace in the hurly-burly of diplomacy, and that he always carried a good catalogue or two in his dispatch case. 'He dropped no bricks,' Fred Adams said, 'he mentioned The Grolier Club seventeen times and never called it "Society" once.' It was a great trip!

And, as you can imagine, it was pretty hard settling down—or thinking of going anywhere else again. But there was another very successful trip to California (San Francisco and Los Angeles) in April 1961. I could not go, alas, and neither could Alexander Davidson. (Sadly, he had to resign that year as Club librarian because of illness.)

The next year, 1962, as many of you remember, was the excursion to Italy during three weeks in May—the famous 'Iter Italicum.' Don had become president in 1961 and in the summer of that year we made a 'trial run' with Frank Crome, checking routes, hotels, restaurants, and planning the Club's library visits with two important bookmen, Commendatore de Marinis (aged eighty-four) and young Carlo Alberto Chiesa, once his protégé—both indefatigable and devoted to the cause. Between them they knew every celebrated library in Italy and every person connected with books. The Commendatore promised to prepare little catalogues describing what we would be seeing in the great libraries. His friend Giovanni Mardersteig would print them. 'Collectors' items,' he said. And they are.

After the 'trial run' in the autumn of 1961, Don arranged for a series of talks by Grolier members, who were experts, on Italian cities, Italian libraries, Italian collectors. And on a less fascinating but essential side, we worked on the endless logistics and details of the trip, which involved 130 members (including ladies) in Milan, as many as 150 at other points, with ninety-two scheduled for the plane. We drew numbers out of Don's hat to assign the seats fairly (sixteen in first class, the rest in the economy section). Finally, Saturday 5 May arrived, and we took off on the Grolier Swiss Air charter plane after posing for a group picture in front of the 'Ex Libris' banner and after losing the company of one member whose passport had expired—he would have to follow on Monday (incredibly, this disaster had also occurred on the flight to England, not to the same member, of course).

I have no recollection of 'Grolier watching' on the trip to Italy; I was too busy with this thing and that and trying hopelessly to obey Donald's command not to get out of his sight. One more tragedy did occur before we reached Paradise: a distinguished Grolier member, accustomed to traveling first class, found that he and his lady were seated in the noisiest, most congested, carousing spot on the plane—by the bar and the lavatories. He resigned from the Club in the middle of the night—at thirty thousand feet—and the new librarian, Terry Bender, in distress, reported the bad news to the sleepless president. (After a few days' absence, the member returned to the fold, I am glad to say.) But, oh, at ten o'clock in the morning of 6 May, how glad I was to see the Milan airport and Frank Crome and Mrs. Teague and Carlo Alberto and Elena Chiesa—and four buses.

The marvelous trip began. Milan and hours at the Ambrosiana Library . . . books and manuscripts lying on tables unprotected, and we were urged to turn the pages, even of the *Codex Atlanticus* with over a thousand drawings by Leonardo!

Verona . . . the Capitolare Library . . . where Monsignore Turrini, the librarian, and Mr. Creswick, the Cambridge University librarian, carried on a conversation—in Latin. The noonday banquets at the villas of the Galtarossas and the Fagiuolis . . . and later a tour of the Mardersteig Press.

Everywhere we went we gave hosts presents, copies of *Grolier 75* and of Waller Barrett's *Italian Influence on American Literature*. Don asked various members, usually a day ahead, to prepare a little presentation speech: Vice President Bob Taylor, Secretary Fritz Liebert, Treasurer Al Howell, John Crawford, Morris Saffron, and others. Fourteen of the group, we discovered, spoke Italian of various sorts: Waller used the language of Dante, Barney Rosenthal was perfectly bilingual, and Gabriel Austin had a Sicilian accent. This young man, on holiday from the New York Public Library, became more and more helpful with the running of the trip, and in the following year he became curator of The Grolier Club, and, in 1965, librarian.

Everyone spoke a few words of Italian by the time we reached Venice, and there Commendatore de Marinis was waiting. He supervised the Grolier inspection of the Marciana Library. Count Cini presided over the visit to the magnificent Fondazione Cini, and he issued an invitation to all Grolier members to come to his Foundation and do research.

On to Cesena and the famous Malatesta Library, where we all looked very medieval pouring over the chained books. And has any traveler forgotten the lunch at the restaurant in Cesena where live goldfish swam in the finger bowls!

Then Florence and the Laurenziana and the National Library and I Tatti, and museums shown by their directors, and the great lunch party to the roll of drums at Fort Belvedere, followed immediately by the reception at the de Marinises' Villa Montalto, where they asked four hundred eminent Florentines to meet the Grolier members. And *I know I* shall *never*, *never* forget the reception given at the Palazzo Vecchio by the 'Communist' mayor who charmed us all and who fervently kissed Il Presidente!

All too soon . . . the private train to Naples . . . libraries and museums and also excursions . . . Herculaneum, Pompeii, Salerno, Paestum, and Caserta . . . and through the buses Fritz Liebert's loose-leaf books of postcards were circulated, familiar views and classical objects with 'appropriate' Grolier titles. Rare collection!

We hurried on . . . the private train back to Rome, where the great high spots were the magical evening at the Villa Madama—Cardinal Tisserant in dazzling cardinal red, the Grolier party in 'abito scuro' (as prescribed). Next morning the Vatican Library—Cardinal Tisserant the host—and no request denied. Finally, the banquet given for us by the Grolier Vander Poels at the Castel Sant 'Angelo (by special permission of the Italian government). A starlit sky above the Tiber and the castle edged by a thousand flambeaux provided a proper conclusion to the 'Iter Italicum.'

Wonderful trip—infinite pleasure! After which Don came home to face serious Grolier problems. 'The great refurbishing' of the clubhouse was underway. Fred Adams was chairman of the Building Committee, Arthur Holden the architect—and certainly no job in Arthur's distinguished career received more of his constant and minute attention. A balcony, with bookshelves, was being added in the librarian's office. Chairman Herbert Cahoon and his Library Committee were putting all the Club's valuable books and catalogues into proper condition, discarding irrelevant material, and making acquisitions with the generous Harper Fund; the committee's goal was to have 'the finest bibliographical reference collection in the country.' Don was working hard on the Fund Drive, determined to put the house in order and the Club itself on a sound financial basis. The Council created a new committee, 'Finance,' and was clever enough to make Edward Naumburg its chairman.

From my vantage point the Grolier year of 1963 was chaos. For eight months the clubhouse was out-of-bounds for members. Almost every storey was under construction. To reach their apartment, the Lovetts had to use the elevator of the building next door (now Blimpie's) and go over the roof and down through a hatch.

It seemed to me that when Don was not at his office he was always at the Club. Any time he was home, he was on the telephone, trying to solve the latest Grolier crisis. One day, according to the House Committee chairman, Harrison Horblit, Don was in the exhibition hall, 'surrounded, submerged, by chairs, pictures, couches, bookcases, carpets, clocks, and the like,' when a stranger wandered in from the street. The stranger turned out to be an inspector from the New York Fire Department, who threatened to remove the Club's permit as a public meeting place if this room were not cleaned up in three days. It was—the president assisting and even his lady.

And right after this, Harrison recalls, when the new elevator cab was being installed, the alarm bells went off. No one paid any attention until shouts were also heard. Then, by manipulating the switches, the elevator was brought to a landing and the trapped individual emerged—none other than the president.

Don seemed possessed by his affection for the Grolier. He was involved in every phase of the decoration: painting the rooms, polishing the floors, restoring the furniture, improving the light fixtures, and repairing the clocks. He persuaded the Council to purchase china worthy of the 'renewed' clubhouse; he succeeded in urging one member to replenish the silver and another to donate proper glass for the Council meetings.

As a reward, and perhaps for temporary relief, in May 1963, Don led fifty members (including ladies) on a splendid trip to the Middle West with a glimpse of the South. The group journeyed to Cincinnati, Detroit, Indiana University, the University of Michigan, and, under the aegis of member Larry Thompson, to the University of Kentucky, where member Frank Francis rededicated a library and both Francises and Hydes were made Kentucky Colonels!

By the end of 1963 'the great refurbishing' was completed and, miraculously, the Thursday of the annual meeting in January 1964 fell on the exact eightieth anniversary of Founders' Day, 23 January. Don told me when he came home late that night that there had been resounding applause for all involved in the 'refurbishing,' also a special salute to Lovett on his fortieth anniversary as Club steward, and much applause as well when it was reported that there was now a waiting list for both resident and nonresident membership.

In mid-May 1964, a Grolier auction was held at Parke-Bernet to push forward the Fund Drive, which was still short of its goal. Members rallied for the occasion from near and far; the most eminent out-of-town member was certainly Cardinal Tisserant. He had never been to a book auction before, and he enjoyed it enormously and also enjoyed seeing his Grolier friends again.

A few days after the auction, the Gala Book Week took place. All former hosts in this country, in England, France, and Italy were invited to come and see the 'renascent' clubhouse and to enjoy events in New York City and its environs. Of the more than one hundred guests, nine came from abroad (including three Fagiuolis from Verona). And past hosts from all sections of this country came from Boston, Philadelphia, and Washington, D.C., from Virginia, Michigan, and Kentucky, and—the largest number of all—from California. It was a memorable week: receptions at the Club, at the Morgan Library, at the New York Public, at the Frick; excursions to the Cloisters, a cruise around Manhattan, a day at the World's Fair, an evening with the marvelous horses of the Vienna Riding School; a day at Yale, and the final morning in Princeton, with the afternoon at Four Oaks Farm. We borrowed the Grolier flag to fly that day!

The next thing I knew it was January 1965, and Don was conducting his last annual meeting at the Grolier. He seemed sad when he left for the Club and I was sad too. '30 Sutton Place later,' I have on my calendar and I can tell you, it was a very large, very nostalgic, very late party.

A month later, at the February Council meeting in 1965, Don's term as president came to an end. And so did my days of very, very close 'Grolier watching.'

I still continued to watch from afar, of course—admiringly—the strong presidencies of Gordon Ray (1965–69), Al Howell (1969–73), Bob Taylor (1973–75), and the beginning of Fritz Liebert's term in 1975. I imagined that I would go on 'Grolier watching' as long as I lived.

But in May 1976—suddenly—though I am now told it was the result of 'much diplomatic preparation,' the Council made it possible for qualified ladies to become Grolier Club members.

So now I, and all like me, are no longer 'watching'—we are WORKING—and I hope that the founders, Messieurs Andrews, De Vinne, Drake, Gallup, Hoe, Ives, Marvin, Mead, and Turnure—enjoying their better life—are even a little pleased.

The Evolving Role of Bibliography, 1884–1984

G. THOMAS TANSELLE

In 1886—two years after the founding of The Grolier Club—Percy Fitzgerald, writing of bibliographies in his volume *The Book Fancier*, said, 'Bibliography being a matter on which large sums are invested and study and labour expended, has become almost scientific, with its systems and methods and tests' (p. 94). This statement has a modern ring, for bibliography today involves considerable expense; and whether or not one wishes to call it scientific, it commands a wide array of 'systems and methods and tests.' Yet, with some important exceptions, the bibliographical work of a century ago looks rather rudimentary now; the methods that Fitzgerald refers to would seem, for the most part, unsophisticated to us. On a retrospective occasion such as this, it is pleasing to recognize that we have made advances; but Fitzgerald's comment also reminds us that we have no grounds for complacency, since historians a century hence will see shortcomings in work that we now take pride in. Nevertheless, the achievements of the past century in the field of bibliography are substantial and impressive. Whether or not they will be superseded is less important than the knowledge that they have played a useful role in the continuing process. As we review some of the events of this century, we should be alert to the challenges, still to be satisfactorily met, that they leave in their wake.

The Grolier Club began, not coincidentally, at a time of particular significance in the history of bibliography. What was happening is perhaps symbolized by the fact that Henry B. Wheatley's *How to Form a Library*—another publication of 1886—was dedicated to Henry Bradshaw, who had died in February of that year. Wheatley's book was the first in a series he edited for the publisher Elliot Stock, 'The Book-Lover's Library,' which eventually extended to twenty-five volumes. This series catered to a growing popular interest in book collecting, increasingly at this time manifested in the collecting of recent—that is, nineteenth-century—authors. Invoking Bradshaw's name suggested a link with the scholarly study of the earliest printed books, for Bradshaw was the foremost incunabulist of his time and the one regarded as the founder of a 'scientific' approach to the analysis of physical evidence in books, the so-called 'natural history method' of identifying the printer of a book through an examination of its type. Despite this association, the growth of first-edition collecting developed for a time independently of the tradition of typographical analysis. The 1880s saw the first large flurry in the unending succession of author bibliographies, but it seemed largely unconnected with the other strand of bibliographical endeavor in these years, represented by the appearance of the periodical *The Library* (1888) and of Francis Jenkinson's edition of Bradshaw's *Collected Papers* (1889), by the founding of the bibliographical societies in Edinburgh (1890) and London (1892), and by Samuel Sandars's institution of a series of bibliographical lectures at Cambridge (1894). A major theme in the story of twentieth-century bibliography is the gradual joining of the analytical approach with the effort to record the printed output of particular writers—a beginning recognition of the connections between physical evidence and intellectual content.

If this recognition has reached its fullest expression thus far in a series of scholarly editions in recent decades, I venture to say that all the other significant developments in bibliography over the past century are also witnesses to the same point. A glance at some of the accomplishments in three areas will serve, I think, to characterize the growth of bibliographical understanding that has occurred since 1884 and to show that a single impulse can be discerned running through these parallel histories. One area of important achievement is obviously bibliographical description and the writing of author bibliographies, as evidenced by the contrast between the checklists of the 1880s and such recent books as David Gilson's *Jane Austen* (1982) and Dan H. Laurence's *Bernard Shaw* (1983). Another is certainly the production of those vast works that have come to be known as 'short-title catalogues,' following the precedent set by the Bibliographical Society's most famous publication. And third is analytical bibliography, a field not without its share of controversy but one that is basic to all study of books, as the strides it has taken in the twentieth century make amply clear. The developments in these three areas have repeatedly demonstrated the interdependence of all bibliographical work and the inseparability of collecting and scholarship.

The tradition of separately published single-author bibliographies is not much more than a century old, and it began as an accompaniment to a new approach to book collecting. The kind of collecting celebrated by the founding of the Roxburghe Club (1812) and by the voluminous writings of Thomas Frognall Dibdin, and reflected in the manuals of Thomas Hartwell Horne (*An Introduction to the Study of Bibliography*, 1814) and John Hill Burton (*The Book-Hunter*, 1862), focused on incunabula and early monuments of typography, illustration, and binding. In the last quarter of the nineteenth century, however, stimulated by the example of Locker-Lampson (especially after the publication of his Rowfant catalogue in 1886) and by the formation of numerous literary societies devoted to individual authors (the Wordsworth, Browning, and Shelley societies were all products of the 1880s), many collectors began seeking first editions of literary works, particularly of nineteenth-century English poets— a story chronicled incisively and inimitably by John Carter in *Taste & Technique in Book-Collecting* (1948). The most prolific bibliographer to respond to this movement in the early years was Richard Herne Shepherd, whose *Tennysoniana* appeared as early as 1866 and who proceeded to treat Ruskin, Dickens, Carlyle, Thackeray, and Swinburne before the mid-eighties. His books were only brief checklists, with little physical detail, as were the bibliographies by Charles Plumptre Johnson (Thackeray, Dickens, 1885), John P. Anderson (attached to biographies of Rossetti, Dickens, the Brontës, Scott, Byron, and George Eliot between 1887 and 1890), F. J. Furnivall (in the Browning Society *Papers*, 1881–84), and others who sought to provide the members of the literary societies with (in Michael

Sadleir's words) 'a blend of bibliographical detail and literary information nicely adapted to their needs' (*The Bibliographical Society, 1892–1942*, p. 150). An American equivalent—and the earliest American bibliography of this kind—was *The Longfellow Collectors' Hand-Book*, published anonymously in 1885 by Beverly Chew, a member of The Grolier Club elected just after its founding. The first advance came with H. Buxton Forman's *A Shelley Library* in 1886, which provided fuller detail than its predecessors and which served as a model for Thomas J. Wise, whose long series of bibliographies and catalogues began a few years later with a bibliography (1889–90) of Ruskin (largely the work of J. P. Smart) and continued for more than four decades. In addition to the other crimes of which Wise has now been convicted, he must be reckoned a bad bibliographer, for he was interested less in discovering truth than in promoting his own copies: Simon Nowell-Smith, in a judicious assessment of Wise as a bibliographer, remarks that Wise 'tended to see all his freaks as swans' (*Library*, 5th ser., 24 [1969], 138). Nevertheless, through the force of what was then a formidable reputation and the overwhelming succession of so many elaborate volumes, Wise played an important role in establishing the author bibliography as a genre.

His bibliographies, however, like those that preceded them, were quite superficial and were therefore in marked contrast to the scholarly bibliographical works being produced at the same time by the incunabulists, by a man like Robert Proctor, for example, who was brilliantly working through the implications of Bradshaw's approach. Many people—including many who should have known better—seemed to believe that recent books did not require the kind of detailed study devoted to early books. Even a bibliographer as thoughtful as Falconer Madan based his famous concept of 'degressive bibliography' (in the Bibliographical Society's *Transactions*, 9 [1906–08], 53–65) on the notion that the date of a book determines the length of description to be accorded it, with the shortest accounts being appropriate for modern literature. It is not surprising, then, that lesser lights, like James Duff Brown in *A Manual of Practical Bibliography* (1906), could complain that the 'natural history method' resulted in unnecessary detail: after all, Brown naively asserted, 'the same editions of a book never vary one from another, save in regard to imperfections or

misplaced sheets or leaves' (pp. 62–63). Such comments exhibit no awareness of the possibility that a description of details not known to vary might
prove useful or of the fact that bibliographical details can be properly understood only when placed in a larger historical and biographical context,
encompassing printing, publishing, and textual history. Author bibliographies as a genre thus began life under circumstances suggesting that collectors had different needs from scholars, needs that could be satisfied by
simple guides rather than careful historical accounts. This condescending
notion even today underlies some of the books that are called bibliographies; but the development of author bibliography as a field is largely the
story of attacking and overcoming this attitude.

Surely the more serious collectors of the late nineteenth and early
twentieth centuries rapidly outgrew the unsatisfactory guides they were
presented with and formed a receptive, if small, audience for the approach
to bibliography championed in the 1920s and later by Michael Sadleir.
There had been a few signs of dissatisfaction from the start. In 1880, for
example, Bernard Quaritch published a little book by Ralph Thomas
(under the anagrammatic pseudonym 'Olphar Hamst') called *Aggravating
Ladies*, fortunately supplied with an explanatory subtitle: 'A List of Works
Published under the Pseudonym of "A Lady," with Preliminary Suggestions on the Art of Describing Books Bibliographically.' Thomas was concerned with, among other things, the tendency to shorten the title-page
wording: 'I never abbreviate,' he says, 'or omit anything from a title-page
without fear and trembling' (p. 20). He obviously understood, even if he
did not clearly explain, the value of fuller description. Similarly, Wise—in
one of his real contributions—emphasized the importance of original condition, even though his reasons had more to do with sentiment than with
historical evidence. In 1912 E. T. Cook, in his bibliography of Ruskin, offered the significant observation, 'A Bibliography . . . contains the life-
history of an author's work' (p. xx). Twelve years later Iolo A. Williams, in
Seven XVIIIth Century Bibliographies, included 'interesting and pertinent
historical facts' and noted typographical peculiarities 'even when these occur in every copy that I have examined of the book in question' (p. 12); he
conceived of his book, in other words, as a historical record, not merely a
listing of points for identification of various printings.

It remained for Michael Sadleir, himself a collector and a publisher, to focus more precisely on the connections between bibliography and publishing history. His Trollope bibliography (1928) is a landmark, for one of its stated purposes was 'to put on record facts as to the methods of Victorian publishing' (p. xi); the bibliographer's work, he said, was 'at once historical and bibliolatrous' (p. 251). Sadleir was not the first to understand that the pleasures of collecting are inseparable from the satisfaction of establishing historical facts, but his example was the most effective early demonstration of the point in connection with modern books. He continued his campaign until the end of his life, notably in his important essay for the Bibliographical Society's fiftieth-anniversary volume in 1945 (*The Bibliographical Society, 1892–1942: Studies in Retrospect*), in which he called for the joining of 'collector-experience' with 'knowledge of publishing practice' in the service of bibliography. His belief that the development of author bibliography could be largely measured by its increasing attention to publishing history still holds true today—especially if we think of the connections between publishing history and literary biography. The year after Sadleir's Trollope bibliography, Frederick A. Pottle produced another landmark in *The Literary Career of James Boswell, Esq.*, in which he said at the outset, 'My aim has been to make a thoroughgoing application of the principles of scientific bibliography to the whole of a literary career, in the conviction that such a study is one of the safest and most fruitful ways of coming to understand the character of the author himself' (p. xviii). Since the time of Sadleir and Pottle there have been such further signposts, along the same road, as Richard L. Purdy's bibliography of Hardy (1954) and Dan H. Laurence's of Shaw (1983). Purdy described his book as 'a biography of Hardy in bibliographical form' (p. vii); and Laurence took up the theme, reflecting on his experience with Shaw, in his Engelhard Lecture (1982, published in 1983), appositely entitled *A Portrait of the Author as a Bibliography*. Still others—such as Ian Willison, in his research for an Orwell bibliography—are presently giving particular thought to this aspect of author bibliography. Some have not yet learned the lesson; but the best of recent bibliographies differ from the bibliographies of a century ago by taking seriously their function as historical and biographical studies—by recognizing, in other words, that collectors and scholars do not need different bibliographies, because they are engaged in the same work.

A parallel development has been the growing sophistication and precision in the technique for recording physical details. The idea of presenting these details in a bibliography of course presupposes that a bibliography is a work of historical scholarship; and indeed the impetus for establishing descriptive procedures came from bibliographers of incunabula and English Renaissance books at a time when the study of modern books was still in a primitive stage. The key figure was A. W. Pollard, whose two pioneer essays of 1906–07—one on 'The Objects and Methods of Bibliographical Collations and Descriptions' (*Library*, 2nd ser., 8 [1907], 193–217) and the other, written with W. W. Greg, on 'Some Points in Bibliographical Descriptions' (*Transactions of the Bibliographical Society*, 9 [1906–08], 31–52)—were offshoots of his work on the first volume of the great *Catalogue of Books Printed in the XVth Century Now in the British Museum* (1908–), which should be regarded as the earliest monument of modern descriptive bibliography. The excellence of the entries in this magisterial work led Greg to observe, some three decades later, that 'the duties of the cataloguer . . . embrace the complete investigation of the material construction of the books enumerated and the whole history of their production'; one must realize, he said, that 'it is this life-history of books that is the true study of the bibliographer' (*The Bibliographical Society, 1892–1942*, p. 27). Building on this base, R. B. McKerrow helped to standardize title-page transcription and signature collation in *An Introduction to Bibliography for Literary Students*, which during the half-century after its publication in 1927 was the most influential introduction to bibliographical thinking. Two more treatments of technique—one by Falconer Madan, Gordon Duff, and Strickland Gibson in the 1920s ('Standard Descriptions of Printed Books,' *Oxford Bibliographical Society Proceedings and Papers*, 1 [1922–26], 55–64) and the other by W. W. Greg in the 1930s ('A Formulary of Collation,' *Library*, 4th ser., 14 [1933–34], 365–82)—set the stage for the appearance in 1949 of Fredson Bowers's *Principles of Bibliographical Description*, which has been the standard ever since. Bowers consolidated the work of his predecessors, provided additional detail, and—most important of all—approached the recording of bibliographical facts as historical scholarship. Following his custom, many people now speak of good bibliographies as having been 'written,' not merely 'compiled.' Since 1949 his book has been supplemented in various ways—especially in two comprehensive statements, Greg's fourth volume (1959) of *A Bibliography of the English Printed Drama to the Restoration* and Allan Stevenson's introduction to the second volume (1961) of the *Catalogue of Botanical Books in the Collection of Rachel McMasters Miller Hunt*—but it remains the central work in its field.

These developing standards were of course both reflected in and promulgated by individual bibliographies. In the pre-Bowers era, there were some author bibliographies besides Sadleir's *Trollope* and Pottle's *Boswell* that stood apart from the rest—such as Geoffrey Keynes's long series (going back to his *Donne* of 1914 and including the Grolier Club *Blake* of 1921), Henrietta C. Bartlett and A. W. Pollard's *Shakespeare* (1916, 1939), Reginald H. Griffith's *Pope* (1922–27), Francis R. Johnson's *Spenser* (1933), William M. Sale's *Richardson* (1936), Hugh Macdonald's *Dryden* (1939), J. E. Norton's *Gibbon* (1940), Anthony J. and Dorothy R. Russo's *James Whitcomb Riley* (1944), and Allen Hazen's *Walpole* (1948). An auspicious event at midcentury was the inauguration of Rupert Hart-Davis's series of Soho Bibliographies, under the aegis of John Carter, John Hayward, William A. Jackson, and A. N. L. Munby, with Allan Wade's *Yeats* (1951). Although volumes of the series have varied considerably, it has played a helpful role in publicizing the techniques of modern bibliographical investigation and has had a powerful influence on the arrangement of material in recent bibliographies. Indeed, another series that sets a relatively high standard reflects its influence: the Pittsburgh Series in Bibliography, which began in 1972, under the general editorship of Matthew J. Bruccoli, with Joseph Schwartz and Robert C. Schweik's *Hart Crane*. A number of notable bibliographies have also been published outside these series during the last three decades, including Norma Russell's *Cowper* (1963), B. C. Bloomfield and Edward Mendelson's *Auden* (1964, 1972), Emily M. Wallace's *William Carlos Williams* (1968), Daniel Heartz's *Pierre Attaignant* (1969), and C. William Miller's *Benjamin Franklin's Philadelphia Printing* (1974). Among the new techniques and concerns illustrated in these works are the grouping of printings into plate families (in William W. Kelly's *Ellen Glasgow* [1964]), the use of the Hinman Collator to distinguish impressions (in

Warner Barnes's *Elizabeth Barrett Browning* [1967]), and the incorporation into bibliographical description of the results of textual collation (in James L. W. West III's *William Styron* [1977]). Collectors sometimes lament the loss of the simple bibliographies of the past; but they would not seriously wish to return to them, for the truth cannot be so simply accommodated. The sophistication of collecting and that of bibliography are of course reciprocal: bibliographies are products of collecting as much as they are guides to it. Although inadequate and oversimplified bibliographies continue to appear in large numbers (produced for the most part by a few publishers who know that libraries will buy them), collectors and scholars will not be satisfied with them and will continue the process, now so well begun, of putting on record the complexities that their enthusiasm has uncovered.

I have concentrated thus far on author bibliographies not only because their rise and development are a significant phenomenon of the past hundred years but also because that story illustrates the growing recognition of the interdependence among all fields of bibliography, and between bibliography and literary and historical studies in the broadest sense. Author bibliographies, however, do not have as large an audience as do more comprehensive listings of books, such as those gathered according to subject or place of printing, or those determined by the contents of particular collections. A few of the bibliographies or bibliographical catalogues that encompass large numbers of authors and books—the British Museum catalogue of fifteenth-century books, for instance, or Greg's work on pre-Restoration drama—offer detailed descriptions; but generally such bibliographies present abbreviated entries. Lists of books with little or no physical detail—so-called 'enumerative bibliographies'—have of course existed for centuries, as we have been reminded by one of the Grolier Club's centennial publications, Bernard H. Breslauer and Roland Folter's *Bibliography: Its History and Development* (1984). Within the century most fields have been supplied with historical records of their literature, ranging from E. C. Bigmore and C. W. H. Wyman's *A Bibliography of Printing* (1880–86)—the second volume of which appeared a few months after the founding of The Grolier Club—to Fielding H. Garrison and Leslie T. Morton's *A Medical Bibliography* (1943)—the fourth edition of which came out last year. The aim of many such books is the listing of *works* rather than *editions*: the emphasis is on intellectual, rather than physical, products. But the authors of these listings often come to recognize, in the course of their study, that this distinction is not easy to maintain and that they cannot divorce from their task the investigation of the printing and publishing history of the works recorded, or the analysis of the physical evidence—present in copies of the editions being listed—which reflects that history. The quantity of detail furnished in entries is therefore a less fundamental feature distinguishing one checklist or bibliography from another than the attitude underlying the choice of detail.

This point is aptly illustrated by the category of reference book that is now called a 'short-title catalogue'—the development of which is surely one of the most significant trends in twentieth-century bibliography. The term, and the concept, first gained currency as a result of the appearance in 1926 of what remains even now the most significant publication of the Bibliographical Society, *A Short-Title Catalogue of Books Printed in England, Scotland, & Ireland, and of English Books Printed Abroad, 1475–1640*. As a record primarily of material printed in a particular area during a particular time, the catalogue naturally emphasized production over subject matter. But only someone thinking of physical evidence would have called the entries in the work 'short titles': they were short, that is, in comparison with the descriptions in a full-fledged bibliography. It is not surprising that the chief inspirer of such a work (in a Bibliographical Society paper of 1918) was A. W. Pollard, whose expertise in the physical analysis of books had been brilliantly demonstrated by his introductory essay to the first volume of the British Museum catalogue of fifteenth-century books. The *STC*—as the *Short-Title Catalogue* is almost universally called—is a landmark in the recording of a national literature, for the entries, brief though they are, emerge from the analysis of book production history as revealed in the items themselves. That enumeration must rest on physical analysis has been further, and most effectively, demonstrated by the revision of the *STC*, which has been in progress since the time of its original publication. The work of Katharine Pantzer in completing the revision started by F. S. Ferguson and W. A. Jackson shows that detailed examination of multiple copies is necessary: the depth of her work has been glimpsed through a series of impressive talks she has given and through the occasional entries in the published revision (one volume of which appeared in 1976) that require, to accomplish their purpose, details not regularly comprehended in the idea of a 'short title.'

Another STC, taking up where the original *STC* leaves off, also represents the tradition of a single individual carrying a large bibliographical work to completion: Donald G. Wing's STC covering 1641–1700 (published 1945–51 and now in course of revision as well). And David F. Foxon single-handedly produced an STC of *English Verse 1701–1750* (1975) that includes signature collations and other physical details. But to proceed in this fashion through the entire output of the eighteenth century, not to mention the nineteenth, would require more Pantzers, Wings, and Foxons than the bibliographical world can reasonably expect. What has made an eighteenth-century STC feasible is the computer, along with the dedication of hundreds of librarians who are willing to examine and report the imprints in their charge. Under the direction of Robin Alston at the British Library, and with Henry Snyder coordinating the work in the United States, the ESTC has made remarkable progress in recent years toward the goal—perhaps achievable by the beginning of the 1990s—of providing a comprehensive record, in the form of a computer data base, of the several hundred thousand eighteenth-century imprints in English, offering a considerable number of physical details based, whenever possible, on the reports of a large number of copies. One by-product is the 1983 publication—in microfiche and in the data base of the Research Libraries Information Network (RLIN)—of a catalogue of the British Library holdings (some 150,000 items), all newly described. Another is the reexamination of all American eighteenth-century imprints, under the supervision of Marcus A. McCorison at the American Antiquarian Society—which amounts to a revision of another of the great bibliographical works by a single person, Charles Evans's *American Bibliography* (1903–55)—and their inclusion in the RLIN record.

The existence of computer networks, like RLIN, through which libraries can make their holdings known, dramatically illustrates the progress that has been made since the early days of The Grolier Club. That the catalogues of great libraries or collections are important bibliographical reference works was of course recognized all along, and a few of them were made available in printed form: the *General Catalogue* of the British Museum, for example, began publication in 1881 and the catalogue of the Bibliothèque Nationale in 1897. The development of techniques for facilitating the photographic reproduction of card catalogues in book form resulted in the third quarter of the twentieth century in the publication of the catalogues of many specialized libraries and collections. It is fitting that the largest such undertaking was being completed during the years that saw the beginning of the computer projects: *The National Union Catalog: Pre-1956 Imprints*, its 754 volumes surely constituting the largest reference work ever published in book form, was finished (with appropriate festivities at the Library of Congress) in 1981 and serves now as perhaps the most basic of all bibliographical guides. Its publication marks the end of an era: the computer networks will provide the union catalogues of the future. The advantages that computers offer for handling masses of data have stimulated activity on additional STCs: an NSTC, covering books published in English-speaking countries (and English-language books and translations of them published elsewhere) from 1801 to 1918, based at first on the holdings of six British and Irish libraries; and an ISTC, covering all incunabula and being edited by Lotte Hellinga at the British Library from a base provided by Frederick R. Goff's census of American copies (published by the Bibliographical Society of America in 1964, with a supplement following in 1972). A related union catalogue is the EIP, the Early Imprints Project, which aims to record all pre-1801 imprints in Australian and New Zealand collections. The computer not only facilitates the construction of such catalogues but also provides their users with the possibility of searching the record from a great variety of angles. Not all cataloguers, of course, will prepare their entries for a computer network with the same elaboration; but the fact that some provision is being made, in codes for machine-readable cataloguing, for the retrieval of various details of book-production history presages a very different future for bibliographical research. The idea of acquiring with ease a list of books of a particular genre printed in a certain area during a given year—and perhaps of a particular format and in contemporary binding—no longer strikes bibliographers as wishful thinking. That it does not is one measure of the distance bibliography has traveled over the last century.

Another is suggested by the number and the sophistication of discussions of physical evidence found in bibliographical journals and monographs. One of the interesting phenomena of twentieth-century scholarship is the remarkable development of what has come to be called analytical bibliography. Analysis, at least in some degree, must precede description and classification, and those writing descriptive bibliographies and short-title catalogues must engage in analysis of the evidence before them; but many others, not working on formal bibliographies or catalogues, have also attempted to elucidate the history of certain books by examining some of their physical characteristics. Books, like other artifacts, inevitably contain clues to their own history, and our knowledge of book production must be grounded on the surviving products themselves. This kind of evidence has been most fully exploited by scholars in the English-speaking world, the tradition effectively beginning with Bradshaw's and Proctor's work identifying the printers of incunabula. The monument of Proctor's labors, *An Index to the Early Printed Books in the British Museum* (1898–99), was arranged so that books were grouped together chronologically under their printers (the order of the printers also being chronological under the towns in which they worked, the towns in turn ordered by the dates of the establishment of printing in them). The principle underlying this arrangement, which came to be called 'Proctor order,' is that a book—its physical features no less than its intellectual content—must be examined in its historical context if it is to yield its secrets. Those who ask the computer to furnish a chronological list of the imprints of a particular locality are following in Proctor's path, as are those who decide that a library should maintain an imprint file.

The link to the next step in the history of analytical bibliography was provided by A. W. Pollard, whose influence on twentieth-century bibliography is pervasive. The year after his introduction to the British Museum catalogue of fifteenth-century books, he published another epoch-making work, *Shakespeare Folios and Quartos* (1909), applying to books of a later period the same scrupulous attention to physical details and printing practice. By this time Greg and McKerrow had just begun to set new standards in the editing of Elizabethan texts, showing in the process the role of bibliographical analysis in textual criticism. Under this triumvirate, Renaissance drama then became the field where the most exciting developments in analytical bibliography took place, and it continued to be so for much of the twentieth century. McKerrow's classic and still valuable *Introduction to Bibliography for Literary Students* of 1927 (expanded from his 'Notes on Bibliographical Evidence' in *Transactions of the Bibliographical Society*, 12 [1911–13], 213–318) taught the analytical approach to several generations of scholars; and it was the generation that came to maturity at the time of the Second World War that produced the next major landmarks. In 1948 Fredson Bowers founded the annual *Studies in Bibliography*, which stimulated and published a new wave of bibliographical work. His own book *Bibliography and Textual Criticism* (1964) and Charlton Hinman's *The Printing and Proof-Reading of the First Folio of Shakespeare* (1963) are the central documents of a sizable scholarly industry that uses such tools as the analysis of the recurrence of identifiable types and headlines to try to establish the page-by-page history of the typesetting, proofreading, and printing of individual volumes. There has been less work on books of later periods, but a notable start on the eighteenth century has been made by William B. Todd and Kenneth Povey, among others. For the nineteenth century, the Sadleir circle—largely members of the book trade—made important contributions in the second quarter of this century to an understanding of what Sadleir called 'book structure.' Two members of this group, John Carter and Graham Pollard, were responsible for the most remarkable bibliographical event of the time, exactly fifty years ago: the exposure of what we now know to be the forgeries of Buxton Forman and T. J. Wise in *An Enquiry into the Nature of Certain Nineteenth Century Pamphlets* (1934)—a work that showed the value of attention to physical evidence, both type and paper, in books of recent times.

In 1969 D. F. McKenzie dampened the spirits of some bibliographers with his now-famous essay 'Printers of the Mind' (in *Studies in Bibliography*), which showed that the conclusions reached in certain instances of bibliographical analysis were unfounded and which urged bibliographers to come back to earth by examining the surviving archives of printing and publishing firms. Such admonitions of caution are always welcome reminders of the limitations of inductive reasoning; but the effort, however difficult it is, to understand the evidence preserved in the books themselves must obviously continue, for that evidence—and not what is written about the books in archives—is the primary evidence. Excellent work in the analysis of such evidence does in fact continue at present. In 1983—the twentieth anniversary of Hinman's great book—Peter W. M. Blayney published a similar treatment of the first quarto of *King Lear* (as the first volume of *The Texts of King Lear and Their Origins*, actually dated 1982). At about the same time Paul Needham brought out the first stage of his study of the *Catholicon* (in *Papers of the Bibliographical Society of America*, 76 [1982], 395–456)—which confirms the fact, adumbrated by the work of Allan Stevenson (particularly his use of paper as evidence) and of Wytze and Lotte Hellinga, that fifteenth-century studies are once again in the mainstream of developments in analytical bibliography. Another sign of the future is also associated with incunabula: Richard N. Schwab and an interdisciplinary group of scholars at the Davis campus of the University of California, concentrating thus far on pieces of fifteenth-century printing, are exploring the uses of the cyclotron in the chemical analysis of paper and ink (see *Papers of the Bibliographical Society of America*, 77 [1983], 285–315).

Bibliography is of course a branch of historical study, as I hope these cross-currents I have singled out from a century of endeavor help to illustrate. They are not independent of other historical researches relating to the book: studies of type design, typefounding, papermaking, printing-press manufacture, printing, publishing, bookselling, book collecting, and reading furnish the background for the examination of individual books, and concurrently many of the details on which these studies are based derive from that same examination, or reports of it in works of descriptive and analytical bibliography. Nor is it surprising that leading bibliographical scholars—such as McKerrow, Greg, and Bowers—have been involved in the editing of texts or that some of the best bibliographical work in recent years has appeared in the essays attached to scholarly editions (such as those published under the auspices of the Center for Scholarly Editions of the Modern Language Association of America): establishing texts requires more than bibliography, but bibliography is essential to it, uncovering physical facts that set limits to literary speculation. The historical study of the role of books in society must naturally take into account the textual content of books, which in turn is affected by the processes of production by means of which those books come into being. Despite these interconnections, scholars focusing on one aspect of book history often work in isolation from those investigating another aspect. A central task for the future is the promotion of a genuine understanding, among all concerned with the history of books, of the way in which their studies mesh. The issue is not—as it has sometimes seemed to be recently—whether the search for evidence within books is more, or less, valuable than the search for evidence in printers' records and other documents external to the books. All evidence must obviously be sought out. What is crucial for future progress is the wider recognition that every copy of a printed edition, like every manuscript document, is a separate piece of historical evidence and that even the broadest studies of the influence of books are tied to the basic fact that texts may vary among copies of a single edition.

The best collectors have understood—sometimes consciously, sometimes not—that they are engaged in preserving historical evidence. A generation before The Grolier Club was founded, John Hill Burton, in *The Book-Hunter* (1862), remarked that 'the collector and the scholar are so closely connected with each other that it is difficult to draw the line of separation between them' (p. 108). The statement still stands, but with an added meaning. Burton was thinking of the knowledge that comes from reading the contents of old books; but as a result of bibliographical study in the English-speaking world during the past century, we also see the scholarship of collectors in their reading of the physical forms of books, in their reconstructing of the printing and publishing histories of particular works, and in their understanding of the relations among various texts of those works. Bibliography, in linking physical form with intellectual content, has shown the basic unity of all study of the history of books. The connoisseurship of collecting—or what John Carter called 'taste and technique'—is, we now see, a recognition of the immense significance of the physical characteristics of books. The achievement of Anglo-American bibliography is effectively to have begun the exploration of this truth; it remains for the future to pursue it in such a way as to draw together the efforts of all who wish to understand the ideas that have been conveyed through books.

Scholarship and Readersh
New Directions in the Hi:

ROBERT DARNTON

Let me say at the outset how grateful I am to be invited to speak to you and how much I look forward to a good debate about all aspects of the study of the book—collecting, bibliography, history, and more that is to come.

But my assignment is to provide a report on the state of play in book history. In a word, it's booming. It is an exciting field, one that is old and new at the same time. Its pedigree goes back to the beginnings of modern bibliography in the nineteenth century, yet its rebirth as a variety of social history took place only a few years ago. It has grown so fast in its present form that it has already entered adolescence and is facing new questions about its scholarly identity. How will it define its boundaries over and against older and more established fields? I should confess that I favor as much border crossing as possible, but I think it useful to try to understand what makes a field cohere. So I would like to discuss the relations between book history and the neighboring disciplines of literature and history in general.

Let's begin with a quick look at some recent developments in literary theory. I say 'quick' because, as you know, the theory is flying thick and fast these days, and the first impulse of the layman is to run for cover. But beneath the prolegomena, manifestoes, and discourses on method lies a common tendency, which one can spot among textual critics everywhere—

Hans Robert Jauss and Wolfgang Iser in Germany, Roland Barthes and Tzvetan Todorov in France, and Jonathan Culler and Stanley Fish in this country. Despite their disagreements, they share a conception of literature that may sound rather inimical to the members of The Grolier Club. It is the notion that literature does not exist in libraries, or even in collections, or even in texts. Literature is something that happens every time a reader reads a book. It's an activity—in fact, the act of reading. So we have a new New Criticism, one that usually goes under the rubric Reader Response.

Rather than going into these theories in detail, let me give you one example of how they work. Consider the opening lines of *A Farewell to Arms* as discussed by Walter Ong: 'In the late summer of that year we lived in a house in a village that looked across the river and the plain to the mountains. In the bed of the river there were pebbles and boulders, dry and white in the sun, and the water was clear and swiftly moving and blue in the channels.' You recognize the marks of Hemingway's style right away, but Ong asks some interesting questions about this passage. 'That year,' said Hemingway. 'What year?' asked Ong. 'The river,' said Hemingway. 'What river?' asked Ong. Of course, we're not told; that's the whole point. Hemingway's rhetoric assumes that we already know. Hemingway makes his reader an insider. He casts us in the role of a companion-in-arms who is going to accompany the hero throughout the narrative. In order to 'get' the narrative, to read the book, we have to play this role. We must become the implicit reader created by Hemingway's rhetoric—a new rhetoric that produced a break with earlier narrative conventions—Jane Austen's, for example. This concentration on the way readers respond to rhetoric is, I submit, an important development in literary scholarship. But I think it has one flaw—namely (and here speaks the historian) anachronism. The literary critics assume that people in the past responded to texts the way they, the literary critics, do. And so we have a distinguished cast of twentieth-century professors projecting their sensitivity onto readers in Shakespeare's London and Pascal's Paris. This will not do, yet this is the point where a juncture can be made between literary theory and the history of the book.

Consider one of the most important recent contributions to book history, *The Cheese and the Worms*, by Carlo Ginsburg. Ginsburg ran into an extraordinary document—you'll find that book historians often begin by stumbling on discoveries in archives—the interrogation of a miller named Menocchio by the Inquisition in sixteenth-century Friuli. The Inquisitor sat down and grilled this man of the people about all of his heresies. In the course of the examination, he found out a great deal about what the miller had read. Ginsburg extracted eleven titles from the interrogation and then went back and read the books himself. But he found that the texts differed significantly from Menocchio's version of them. The miller had infused his own ideas into the works, reading actively instead of merely accepting the arguments as they appeared on the page. By, as it were, subtracting the orthodox arguments from Menocchio's 'mis'readings of them, Ginsburg identified a cultural gap, which he went on to associate with popular notions of cosmology. Hence the theme of the cheese and the worms. Menocchio believed that the universe came into existence by a process of spontaneous generation, just as maggots appear in cheese. He held to a radical variety of materialism that seems to have spread quite widely among the common people of Italy in the sixteenth century. It seems that the common reader four centuries ago did not simply take whatever literature was offered to him. He read into his books as much as he read out of them, and by seeing how he read one can understand how he made sense of the world.

I ran into a real reader from eighteenth-century France in the course of my own explorations of the archives. Named Jean Ranson, he was a merchant from La Rochelle and an impassioned Rousseauist. Ranson did not merely read Rousseau and weep: he incorporated Rousseau's ideas in the fabric of his life, as he set up business, fell in love, married, and raised his children. Reading and living run parallel as leitmotifs in a rich series of letters that Ranson wrote between 1774 and 1785 and that show how Rousseauism became absorbed in the way of life of the provincial bourgeoisie under the Old Regime. Rousseau had received a flood of letters from readers like Ranson after the publication of *La Nouvelle Héloïse*. It was the first tidal wave of fan mail, I believe, in the history of literature. The mail reveals that readers everywhere in France responded as Ranson did and, furthermore, that their responses conformed to those Rousseau had called for in the two prefaces to his novel. He had instructed his readers how to read him. He had assigned them roles and provided them with a strategy for taking in his novel. They were taken in. *La Nouvelle Héloïse* became the greatest best seller of the century, the most important single source of romantic sensibility. That sensitivity is now extinct. No modern reader could weep his way through the six volumes of *La Nouvelle Héloïse* as his ancestors did two centuries ago. But in his day, Rousseau was able to move an entire generation of readers by refashioning reading itself.

Those two examples point in opposite directions. Menocchio illustrates how a reader appropriated a text by deviating from a reading implicit in it, and Ranson shows how a reader adopted a role called for by the rhetoric. Those responses hardly exhaust the possibilities. Two cases cannot provide a beginning for a serious history of reading. But they suggest its possibilities. Although texts may lend themselves to many different and contradictory readings, there are limits to the ways in which they can be read at a given time. Their rhetoric itself sets up constraints, even for those who resist it. And the assumptions peculiar to an era and a social milieu provide a frame of reference for a reader, even for one who 'mis'reads. Textual analysis and archival research can be joined in a common effort to match implicit and actual readers and to study all their metamorphoses.

That kind of history may look utopian now, but historians of the book have already done a great deal of work on the more manageable aspects of the problem—the empirical questions about the 'who,' the 'what,' the 'where,' and the 'when' of reading, which can be of great help in the attempt to attack the more difficult 'whys' and 'hows.'

The 'what' questions fall into two groups, the macro- and micro-analysis of reading habits. Macroanalytical studies depend inevitably upon the available documents, which vary in character and quality from place to place. French historians like Robert Estivals draw on state archives, which contain registers of requests for privileges to publish books running back to the seventeenth century. Germans, led by Johann Gold-friedrich and Rudolf Jentzsch, have relied on the extraordinarily rich catalogues of the book fairs of Leipzig and Frankfurt am Main, which go back to 1594. The British seem to have a distaste for statistics, perhaps because they have concentrated so heavily on descriptive bibliography, but they have produced a remarkable series of short-title catalogues that provide a general view of English literature from 1475 and that have been used effectively by H. S. Bennett, W. W. Greg, and others. In the United States we can draw on Charles Evans's *American Bibliography*. It contains eighteen thousand entries for the period 1638–1783, and its usefulness as a source for spotting general trends in American literature has been demonstrated in the work of G. Thomas Tanselle and Robert B. Winans.

So much effort has gone into the compiling of these statistics that none seems to be left for drawing conclusions or for making comparisons from one country to another. But the evidence itself is neither conclusive nor comparable. What can serve as a valid index to reading habits—French privileges, German book fair catalogues, or English library holdings? Each has drawbacks of its own, and each undercuts the others. The inconsistencies may not be surprising, but they are discouraging: perhaps we shall never be able to produce solid statistics for the prestatistical eras—that is, for all history before the nineteenth century.

Nonetheless, the macroanalytical urge is not to be repressed. It has made most headway in France. In an article written three-quarters of a century ago ('Les enseignements des bibliothèques privées,' *Revue d'histoire littéraire de la France*, 1910) Daniel Mornet asked a fundamental question: What did Frenchmen read in the eighteenth century? He resisted the easy answer—eighteenth-century French literature—because he realized that his notion of that literature was derived from a canon of classics that developed in the nineteenth century. In order to uncover the literature that was actually read, he compiled titles from the auction catalogues of five hundred private libraries. In the end, he accumulated twenty thousand index cards—and how many copies of the *Social Contract* do you think he found? One. Just one reference to the book that was to become the bible of the French Revolution. That finding alone seemed to justify a major overhaul of the standard textbook view of the eighteenth century, and Mornet went on to note that the French of the Old Regime favored best-selling authors like Thémiseul de Saint-Hyacinthe, Mme de Graffigny, and the abbé Pluche, who had subsequently disappeared from literary history. He concluded that history itself had taken a wrong turn, misled by anachronisms and an ideological view of the Revolution: 'C'est la faute à Voltaire, c'est la faute à Rousseau.'

Actually, Mornet made enough false steps of his own to invalidate his conclusions, but his article challenged some of the basic views about French literature. The challenge was taken up again in the 1960s by a group of historians working with François Furet at the Ecole Pratique des Hautes Etudes. They tried to modernize Mornet, and in doing so they produced a series of studies, published in two volumes as *Livre et société dans la France du XVIIIe siècle* (Paris, 1965–70), which has probably been more influential than any other work in the recent revival of book history. The *Livre et société* group also attempted to recover the literature that was actually read in the eighteenth century. They, too, compiled statistics. But they went to different sources: registers of requests for privileges and *permissions tacites*, reviews in literary journals, and even collections of popular chapbooks. In the end, their eighteenth century emerged looking very much like Mornet's. Traditional reading matter, from the chapbooks to the old-fashioned tomes of jurisprudence and devotional literature, outweighed the elements of modernity. 'Inertia' crushed 'innovation.' The Enlightenment, seen from statistics spread over a long stretch of time, looked relatively unimportant.

Like most revisionists, the *Livre et société* group is likely to be revised. For my part, I think Voltaire and Rousseau really were best sellers, and their works were reinforced by those of less distinguished but equally popular writers like Louis Sébastien Mercier and Simon-Henri Linguet. But *Livre et société*, extending the earlier work of Henri-Jean Martin, brought book history into the broad-gauged variety of socio-cultural history associated with the 'school' of the *Annales*. Moreover, many of the charts and graphs in *Livre et société* confirm trends that appear in other sources. In tabulating requests for privileges, Furet found a decline in the older branches of learning, especially the Humanist literature in Latin, that had flourished in the seventeenth century, according to the research of Martin. Newer genres, particularly books classified under the rubric 'sciences et arts,' prevailed in the second half of the eighteenth century. Daniel Roche spotted a similar tendency in his vast survey of Parisian notarial archives. Novels, travel books, and works on natural history tended to crowd out the classics in the libraries of noblemen and wealthy bourgeois. All the studies point to a significant drop in religious literature during the eighteenth century. They confirm the results of quantitative research in other areas of social history—Michel Vovelle's work on funeral rituals and attitudes toward the afterlife, for example, and Dominique Julia's investigation of clerical ordinations and teaching practices.

German studies complement the French. Pietism and humanism dominated northern German culture in the seventeenth century. In the eighteenth century, according to Rudolf Jentzsch and Albert Ward, the fair catalogues of Leipzig and Frankfurt show a marked drop in Latin books and an increase in novels. By the late nineteenth century, according to Eduard Reyer and Rudolf Schenda, borrowing patterns in German, English, and American libraries had fallen into a strikingly similar pattern: 70 to 80 percent of the books came from the category of light fiction (mostly novels); 10 percent from history, biography, and travel; and less than one percent from religion. The world of reading had been secularized. The rise of the novel had balanced a decline in religious literature, and the turning point in every graph came in the second half of the eighteenth century, especially the 1770s, the years of the *Wertherfieber. Die Leiden des jungen Werthers* produced a more spectacular response in Germany than *La Nouvelle Héloïse* had done in France or *Pamela* in England. All three novels marked the triumph of a new literary sensitivity, and the last sentences of *Werther* seemed to announce the advent of a new reading public and the death of an old, pietistic culture: 'Handwerker trugen ihn. Kein Geistlicher hat ihn begleitet.'

Thus the macroanalytic studies do suggest some general conclusions, something like Max Weber's 'demystification of the world.' That may seem too cosmic for comfort. Those who favor precision can turn to microanalysis, although it usually goes to the opposite extreme—excessive detail. We have hundreds of lists of books in libraries from the Middle Ages to the present—more than anyone can bear to read. Yet we would all agree, and especially the members of The Grolier Club, that a library catalogue can be a profile of a reader, even though we don't read all the books we own. To go over the list of the books in Jefferson's library is to inspect the furniture of his mind, and the study of private libraries has the advantage of linking the 'what' with the 'who' of reading.

The French have taken the lead in this area, too. They have produced statistical pictures of the libraries of specific groups—noblemen, magistrates, priests, academicians, burghers, artisans, even some domestic servants. They have also studied reading in certain cities—the Caen of Jean-Claude Perrod, the Paris of Michel Marion—and in whole regions—the Normandy of Jean Quéniart, the Languedoc of Madeleine Ventre. For the most part, they rely on *inventaires après décès*, notarial records of books left after a death. Admittedly, notaries often neglected books of little value or contented themselves with vague remarks such as 'a pile of books.' We can't estimate how much book owning and book reading took place beyond the range of the inquisitive notarial eye. There must have been a great deal of it in northern Europe and America, where notaries were much less important than in the Latin countries. Rudolf Schenda considers inventories woefully inadequate as a guide to reading habits among the common people because in Germany they mention family heirlooms (mainly old Bibles and the pietistic writings of Johann Arndt) rather than current books. If Walter Wittmann's study of inventories in Frankfurt is reliable, the vast majority of the working classes in the late eighteenth century (73 percent of the journeymen and 65 percent of the artisans, as opposed to 49 percent of the tradesmen and zero percent of the higher officials) owned no books at all. Daniel Roche found the same pattern among the common people of Paris: 65 percent of the salaried workers and domestic servants who appear in the notarial archives around 1780 did not own books. But Roche also discovered many indications of familiarity with the written word. By 1789, almost all the domestic servants could sign their names on the inventories. A great many owned desks, fully equipped with writing implements and packed with family papers. Most artisans and shopkeepers spent several years of their childhood in school. Before 1789, Paris had five hundred primary schools, one for every one thousand inhabitants, all more or less free. Parisians were readers, Roche concludes, but reading did not take the form of the books that show up in inventories. It involved chapbooks, broadsides, posters, personal letters, and even the signs on the streets. Parisians read their way through the city and through their lives, but their ways of reading did not leave enough traces for the historian to follow closely on their heels.

He must therefore search out other sources. Subscription lists have been a favorite, though they normally cover only rather wealthy readers. From the late seventeenth to the early nineteenth century, many books were published by subscription in Britain and contained lists of the subscribers. Researchers at the Project for Historical Biobibliography at Newcastle upon Tyne have used these lists to work toward a historical sociology of readership. Similar efforts are under way in Germany, especially among scholars of Klopstock and Wieland. Perhaps a sixth of new German books were published by subscription between 1770 and 1810, when the practice reached its peak. But even during their *Blütezeit*, the subscriptions do not provide an accurate view of readership. They left off the names of many subscribers, included others who never meant to read the book, and generally represented the salesmanship of a few entrepreneurs rather than the reading habits of the educated public, according to some devastating criticism that Reinhard Wittmann has directed against subscription-list research. The work of Wallace Kirsop suggests that such research may succeed better in France, where publishing by subscription also flourished in the late eighteenth century. But the French lists, like all the others, generally favor the wealthiest readers and the fanciest books.

The records of lending libraries offer a better opportunity to make connections between literary genres and social classes, but few of them survive. The most remarkable are the registers of borrowings from the ducal library of Wolfenbüttel, which extend from 1666 to 1928. According to Wolfgang Milde, Paul Raabe, and John McCarthy, they show a significant 'democratization' of reading in the 1760s: the number of books borrowed doubled; the borrowers came from lower social strata (they included a few porters, lackeys, and lower officers in the army); and the reading matter became lighter, shifting from learned tomes to sentimental novels (imitations of *Robinson Crusoe* went over especially well). Curiously, the registers of the Bibliothèque du Roi in Paris show that it had about the same number of users at this time—about fifty a year, including one Denis Diderot. The Parisians could not take the books home, but they enjoyed the hospitality of a more leisurely age. The librarian opened his doors to them only two mornings a week, and before closing he invited them to his table. Book historians have discovered something that economists considered mythical: the free lunch.

No doubt other discoveries are still in store. But the microanalysts have already turned up so much material that they face the same problem as the macroquantifiers: how to put it all together. The disparity of the documentation—auction catalogues, notarial records, subscription lists, library registers—does not make the task easier. And the monographs often cancel each other out: artisans look literate here and unlettered there; travel literature seems to be popular among some groups in some places and unpopular in others. A systematic comparison of genres, milieux, times, and places would look like a conspiracy of exceptions trying to disprove every rule.

So far only one book historian has been hardy enough to propose a general model. Rolf Engelsing has argued that a 'reading revolution' (Leserevolution) took place at the end of the eighteenth century. From the Middle Ages until sometime after 1750, men read 'intensively.' They had only a few books—the Bible, an almanac, a devotional work or two—and they read them over and over again, usually aloud and in groups, so that a narrow range of literature became deeply impressed on their consciousnesses. By 1800, men were reading 'extensively.' They read all kinds of material, especially periodicals and newspapers, and read it only once, then raced on to the next item. Engelsing does not produce much evidence for his hypothesis. Indeed, most of his research concerns only burghers in Bremen. But it has an attractive before-and-after simplicity, and it provides a handy formula for contrasting modes of reading very early and very late in European history. Its main drawback, as I see it, is its unilinear character. Reading did not evolve in one direction, extensiveness. It assumed many different forms. Men read in order to save their souls, to improve their manners, to repair their machinery, to seduce their sweethearts, to learn what was going on in the world, and just to have fun. In many cases, especially among the publics of Richardson, Rousseau, and Goethe, the reading became more intensive, not less. But the late eighteenth century does seem to represent a turning point, a time when more reading matter became available to a wider public, when one can see the emergence of a mass readership that would grow to giant proportions in the nineteenth century with the development of machine-made paper, steam-powered presses, linotype, and nearly universal literacy. All these changes opened up new possibilities, not by decreasing intensity but by increasing variety.

I must therefore confess to some skepticism about the 'Leserevolution.' Yet an American scholar, David Hall, has described a transformation in the reading habits of New Englanders between 1600 and 1850 in almost exactly the same terms as those used by Engelsing. Before 1800, New Englanders read a small corpus of venerable 'steady sellers'—the Bible, almanacs, the *New England Primer*, Philip Doddridge's *Rise and Progress of Religion*, Richard Baxter's *Call to the Unconverted*—and read them over and over again, aloud, in groups, and with exceptional intensity. After 1800, they were swamped with new kinds of books—novels, newspapers, fresh and sunny varieties of children's literature—and they read through them ravenously, discarding one thing as soon as they could find another. Hall and Engelsing had never heard of one another when they published their works. The convergence of their conclusions suggests that a fundamental shift in the nature of reading took place at the end of the eighteenth century. It may not have been a revolution, but it marked the end of an Old Regime.

The 'where' of reading is more important than you might think because by placing the reader in his setting one can begin to approach his experience of the word. In the University of Leyden there hangs a print of the university library, dated 1610. It shows the books, heavy folio volumes, chained on high shelves jutting out from the walls in a sequence determined by the rubrics of classical bibliography: *Jurisconsulti, Medici, Historici*, and so on. Students are scattered about the room, reading the books on counters built at shoulder level below the shelves. They read standing up, protected against the cold by thick cloaks and hats, one foot perched on a rail to ease the pressure on their bodies. Reading cannot have been comfortable in the age of classical humanism. In pictures done a century and a half later, 'La Lecture' and 'La Liseuse' by Fragonard, for example, readers recline in chaises longues or well-padded armchairs with their legs propped on footstools. They are often women, wearing loose-fitting gowns known as *liseuses*. They hold a dainty duodecimo volume in their fingers and have a faraway look in their eyes. From Fragonard to Monet, who also painted a 'Liseuse,' reading moves from the boudoir to the outdoors. The reader backpacks books to meadows and mountaintops, where like Werther and Heine he can commune with nature. Nature must have seemed out of joint a few generations later in the trenches of World War I and the tanks of World War II. These settings hardly left room for the slim volumes of poems brought by the young lieutenants from Göttingen and Oxford. My most precious book is a small edition of Hölderlin's *Hymnen an die Ideale der Menschheit*, inscribed 'Adolf Noelle, Januar 1916, nord-Frankreich'—a gift from a German friend who was trying to explain Germany. I'm still not sure I understand, but I think the general understanding of reading would be advanced if we thought harder about its iconography and accoutrements, including furniture and dress.

The human element in the setting must have affected the understanding of the texts. No doubt Greuze sentimentalized the collective character of reading in his painting of 'Un Père de famille qui lit la Bible à ses enfants.' Restif de la Bretonne probably did the same in the family Bible readings described in *La Vie de mon père*: 'Je ne saurais me rappeler, sans attendrissement, avec quelle attention cette lecture était écoutée; comme elle communiquait à toute la nombreuse famille un ton de bonhomie et de fraternité (dans la famille je comprends les domestiques). Mon père commençait toujours par ces mots: "Recueillons-nous, mes enfants; c'est l'Esprit Saint qui va parler."' But all the evidence indicates that reading was a social activity for the common people everywhere in early modern Europe. It took place in workshops, barns, and taverns; and it was often more *gemütlich* than edifying. Thus the peasant in the country inn described, with some rose tinting around the edges, by Christian Schubart in 1786:

> Und bricht die Abendzeit herein,
> So trink ich halt mein Schöpple Wein;
> Da liest der Herr Schulmeister mir
> Was Neues aus der Zeitung für.

The most important institution of popular reading under the Old Regime was a fireside gathering known as the *veillée* in France and the *Spinnstube* in Germany. While children played, women sewed, and men repaired tools, one of the company who could decipher a chapbook would regale them with the adventures of *Les Quatre fils Aymon* or *Till Eulenspiegel*. Some chapbooks indicated that they were meant to be taken in through the ears by beginning with phrases such as, 'What you are about to hear. . . .' In the nineteenth century, groups of artisans, especially tailors, took turns reading, or hired a reader, to keep themselves entertained while they worked. Even today many people get their news by being read to by a telecaster. Television may be less of a break with the past than is generally assumed. In any case, for most people throughout most of history, books had audiences rather than readers. They were better heard than seen.

Reading was a more private experience for the minority of educated persons who could afford books. But many of them joined reading clubs, *cabinets littéraires*, or *Lesegesellschaften*, where they could read almost anything they wanted, in a sociable atmosphere, for a small monthly payment. Françoise Parent-Lardeur has traced the proliferation of these clubs under the Restoration in Paris, but they went back well into the eighteenth century. Provincial booksellers often turned their stock into a non-circulating library and charged dues for the right to frequent it. Good light, some comfortable chairs, a few pictures on the wall, and subscriptions to a half-dozen newspapers were enough to make a club out of almost any bookshop. If a member liked a book enough, he often bought it. So the *cabinet littéraire* usually helped the trade instead of hurting it. German reading clubs assumed different forms for different publics, but all of them provided a kind of sociability that was crucial to eighteenth-century culture, according to Otto Dann. They sprang up at an astounding rate, especially in the northern cities. Martin Welke estimates that perhaps one of every five hundred Germans belonged to a *Lesegesellschaft* by 1800. Marlies Prüsener has been able to identify well over four hundred of the clubs and to form some idea of their reading matter. All of them offered a rich assortment of periodicals, supplemented by uneven runs of books, usually on fairly weighty subjects like history and politics. They seem to have been a more serious version of the coffeehouse, which spread to Germany from England in the late seventeenth century. By 1760, Vienna had at least sixty coffeehouses. They provided newspapers, journals, and ample opportunity for political discussions, exactly as they did in London and Amsterdam.

Thus we already know a good deal about the institutional bases of reading. We have some answers to the 'who,' 'what,' 'where,' and 'when' questions. But how can we understand the way reading took place in people's minds? I should confess right away that I haven't found a solution to that problem, but I would like to end with some suggestions about ways of tackling it.

First, I think it should be possible to learn more about the ideals and assumptions underlying reading in the past. Old primers and textbooks might reveal notions about the purpose of reading as well as the techniques of doing it. A large literature on the 'art of reading' grew up in the eighteenth and nineteenth centuries. It could be helpful in charting the values connected with the mastery of the printed word. While studying the most important French and German manuals from the period around 1800, *Les vrais principes de la lecture* by N.-A. Viard and *Die Kunst Bücher zu Lesen* by J. A. Bergk, I was surprised to find how completely they agreed: reading was a serious business, to be done for moral improvement rather than for amusement or even the accumulation of knowledge. As a working hypothesis, I would assert that the further back in time you go, the further you move away from instrumental reading. The 'how-to' book becomes rarer and the religious book more common. In the sixteenth and seventeenth centuries, Boccaccio and Rabelais notwithstanding, reading was approached with awe. It was a sacred activity. It put you in the presence of the Word and unlocked holy mysteries. I suspect that the greatest impetus to the spread of reading was the Reformation and the Counter-Reformation rather than the invention of movable type. After those events, the history of reading can be seen as a process of secularization, what I referred to earlier as the demystification of the world.

On the more mundane level, assumptions about reading could be traced through advertisements and prospectuses for books. Thus some typical remarks from an eighteenth-century prospectus taken at random from the rich collection in the Newberry Library: the bookseller is offering a two-volume quarto edition of the *Commentaires sur la coutume d'Angoumois*, an excellent work, he insists, both for its content and its typography: 'Le texte de la *Coutume* est imprimé en gros-romain; les sommaires qui précèdent les commentaires sont imprimés en cicéro; les commentaires sont imprimés en caractères de Saint-Augustin. Tout l'ouvrage est imprimé sur très beau papier d'Angoulême.' When books were made by hand, their physical qualities mattered far more than they do today. Customers in eighteenth-century bookshops sampled the wares the way we might taste wine. They had a typographical consciousness that is now nearly extinct—except, of course, in The Grolier Club.

Censors' reports also can be revealing, at least for the historian of books in early modern France, where censorship was highly developed if not enormously effective. A typical travel book, *Nouveau voyage aux isles de l'Amérique* (Paris, 1722) by J.-B. Labat contains four 'approbations' printed out in full next to the privilege. One censor explains that the manuscript piqued his curiosity: 'J'ai eu du plaisir en le lisant. Il y a une infinité de choses très curieuses.' Another recommends it for its 'style simple et concis' and also its utility: 'Rien à mon avis n'est si utile aux voyageurs, aux habitants de ce pays, aux commerçants, et à ceux qui s'appliquent à l'étude de l'histoire naturelle.' And a third simply found it a good read: 'Il sera difficile d'en commencer la lecture sans éprouver cette douce, quoiqu'avide, curiosité qui nous porte à poursuivre.' Censors did not simply hound out heretics and revolutionaries. They gave the royal stamp of approval to a work, and in doing so they provided clues as to how it might be read. Their values constituted an official standard against which ordinary readings might be measured.

But how did ordinary readers read? My second suggestion for attacking that problem concerns contemporary accounts of reading. Margaret Spufford has uncovered a great many autodidacts from seventeenth-century England and has shown how much reading was learned outside of schools. Pupils inside learned reading before writing. They often joined the work force before age seven, when instruction in writing began. So literacy estimates based on the ability to write may be much too low, and the ability to read may have been much more widespread than we have thought. If Viard's primer represents common practices, children learned to sound out letters, syllables, and words in the eighteenth century pretty much as they do today. They had to memorize a great deal, and they had to demonstrate their mastery of texts by oral performances before the class and the teacher, who never seems to have spared the rod. But practices must have varied a great deal. We still do not know how children learned to read two and three centuries ago. We still do not have a history of experience in the classroom.

If the experience of the great mass of readers lies beyond the range of historical research, historians can recapture something of what reading meant for a few persons, who suggest what it might have meant for others. We can begin with the best-known autobiographical accounts—those of Montaigne, Rousseau, and Stendhal—and move on to less familiar sources. David Hall has found some fascinating reports on reading among his early New Englanders. Daniel Roche discovered an eighteenth-century glazier, Jacques-Louis Ménétra, who read his way around a typical tour de France. Although he did not carry many books in the sack slung over his back, Ménétra constantly exchanged letters with his friends and sweethearts, picked up broadsides, and even composed doggerel verse for the ceremonies and farces that the workers staged in taverns and streets. Ménétra learned to read his life the way he read the map of France. When he put it into words, in one of the most extraordinary working-class autobiographies that exists, he organized it in picaresque fashion, as a series of adventures on the road. His life took on meaning by being placed within a frame—one that combined oral tradition (folk tales and farces recounted in male bull sessions) and the genres of popular literature (the adventure stories of the bibliothèque bleue).

It may be possible to learn what books meant to readers by studying marginalia. All of us have come across modern book graffiti—a regretable variety of vandalism, but an interesting one because they sometimes reveal how readers responded to other readers' responses as well as to the texts. I have learned a great deal from following the dialogue of students in the margins of books kept on reserve in Lamont Library at Harvard University. Christiane Berkvens-Stevelinck is learning far more by studying the marginal notes of Prosper Marchand, the great bibliophile of eighteenth-century Leyden. Scholars have often charted literary currents by tracing them to the margins of rare books—Melville's copy of Emerson, for example, and Napoleon's of Rousseau. But why limit the inquiry to books? Peter Burke is currently studying the graffiti of Renaissance Italy. When scribbled on the door of an enemy, they often functioned as ritual insults, which divided neighborhoods and clans. When attached to the famous statue of Pasquino in Rome, they set the tone of a rich and highly political street culture. A history of reading might be able to make great leaps from the Pasquinade and the Commedia dell'Arte to Molière, from Molière to Rousseau, and from Rousseau to Robespierre.

My third suggestion relates to analytical bibliography. In a study of Congreve, D. F. McKenzie has shown that the playwright had two typographical existences. First came the bawdy, neo-Elizabethan Congreve of the quarto editions from the late seventeenth century; then came the stately, neo-classical Congreve from the three-volume octavo *Works* of 1710. Individual words rarely changed at all, but the text acquired new meaning as a consequence of book design. By adding scene divisions, grouping characters, relocating lines, and bringing out *liaisons des scènes*, Congreve reshaped his plays along classical lines. The early editions do not even distinguish scenes. The late *Works* reveal the articulation of all the parts and show how they fit together in a harmonious whole. To read the two incarnations of the same text is to move from Elizabethan to Georgian England.

Roger Chartier has done a similar study of the metamorphoses of a Spanish classic, *Historia de la vida del Buscón* by Francisco de Quevedo. The novel was originally intended for a worldly and wealthy public, both in Spain where it was first published in 1626 and in France where it came out in a sophisticated translation in 1633. But in the mid-seventeenth century the Oudot and Garnier houses of Troyes began to publish a series of cheap paperback editions, which made it a staple of the popular literature known as the bibliothèque bleue for two hundred years. The popular publishers modified the text, but they especially changed the book design, what Chartier calls the 'mise en livre.' They broke the story into simpler units, shortening sentences, subdividing paragraphs, and multiplying the number of chapters. The new typographical structure implied a new kind of reading and a new public: humble people, who lacked the facility and the time to take in lengthy stretches of narrative. The short episodes were autonomous. They did not need to be linked by complex subthemes and character development because they were just long enough to fill a *veillée*. So the book itself became a collection of fragments rather than a continuous story, and it could be put together by each reader-listener in his own way. Chartier insists on the sociological element in this 'appropriation.' He shows how the implicit reader of the author has moved down the social ladder by becoming the implicit reader of the publisher and how bibliography can open on to social history.

These considerations may be so complex that we will never be able to look back over the whole course of the history of reading. But if we could begin at the beginning, we would have to take note of the fact that the literature of antiquity was not merely memorized and declaimed; it was written and read. But how? How did the Romans decipher the wax tablets or papyrus on which Cicero's speeches were inscribed? We don't know, but we can assume that like most Roman inscriptions, they contained no punctuation, paragraphing, or spacing between words. The units of sound and meaning probably were closer to the rhythms of speech than to the typographical units—the ens, words, and lines—of the printed page.

The page itself as a unit of the book dates only from the third or fourth century A.D. Before then, one had to unroll a book to read it. Once gathered pages (the *codex*) replaced the scroll (*volumen*), readers could easily move backwards and forwards through books, and texts became divided into segments that could be marked off and indexed. Yet long after books acquired their modern form, reading continued to be an oral experience, done aloud and in public. At an indeterminate point, perhaps in some monasteries in the seventh century, and certainly in the universities of the thirteenth century, men began to read silently and alone. The shift to silent reading might have involved a greater mental adjustment than the shift to the printed text, for it made reading an individual, interior experience.

Printing made a difference, of course, but it may have been less revolutionary than is commonly believed. Some books had title-pages, tables of contents, indexes, pagination, and publishers who produced multiple copies from scriptoria for a large reading public before the invention of movable type. For the first half-century of its existence, the printed book continued to be an imitation of the manuscript book. It probably was read by the same public in the same way. But after 1500, the printed book, pamphlet, broadside, map, and poster reached new kinds of readers and stimulated new kinds of reading. Increasingly standardized in its design, cheaper in its price, and widespread in its distribution, the new book transformed the world. It did not simply supply more information. It provided a mode of understanding, a basic metaphor for making sense of life. So it was that during the sixteenth century men took possession of the Word; during the seventeenth century they began to decode the 'book of nature'; and in the eighteenth century they learned to read themselves. With the help of books, Locke and Condillac studied the mind as a tabula rasa, and Franklin formulated an epitaph for himself.

THE BODY OF

B. FRANKLIN, PRINTER,

LIKE THE COVER OF AN OLD BOOK,

ITS CONTENTS TORN OUT,

AND STRIPT OF ITS LETTERING & GILDING

LIES HERE, FOOD FOR WORMS.

BUT THE WORK SHALL NOT BE LOST;

FOR IT WILL, AS HE BELIEV'D,

APPEAR ONCE MORE

IN A NEW AND MORE ELEGANT EDITION

CORRECTED AND IMPROVED

BY THE AUTHOR.

I don't want to flog the metaphor to death but rather to make a point so simple that it may escape our notice: reading has a history. It was not always and everywhere the same. It changed in response to shifts in the underlying organization of texts as well as society. And the cumulative effect of those changes has shaped man's understanding of the cosmos and himself.

This lecture was given as a trial run for a paper to be presented at the George Rudé Seminar in Melbourne in August 1984. In its final form, the paper will contain references and acknowledgments to those who provided help in its preparation.

The Future of the Book

ROBERT GIROUX

Speculating about the future—the future of anything—is a subtle and problematic business. Anyone who has lived long enough into what was once the Future and is now the Past knows how easy it is to guess wrong even about the times immediately ahead. Nevertheless, the temptation to speculate is irresistible. I can recall three experiences I've had with—shall we call it prognostication, or the attempt to anticipate the future, or prophecy? They are experiences that throw light on and are, I believe, relevant to my subject.

The first occurred when I was an undergraduate studying under Mark Van Doren, the poet. He was a great movie fan, as I was, and one day in 1935 we went to see H. G. Wells's film about the future, *Things to Come*. It had an excellent cast—Raymond Massey, Ralph Richardson, Cedric Hardwicke—and was visually brilliant with its futuristic sets, costumes, and space machines designed by Cameron Menzies, the director, who was also a specialist in décor. Wells's script (which I still possess in book form as published in 1935 by Macmillan) turned out to be at least partially accurate as prophecy. It presents a picture of the world from 1936 to 2036, opening with a blitzkrieg version of World War II, which starts on Christmas Eve 1936, followed by the swift downfall of civilization. In the aftermath, the globe is seriously depopulated by a pestilence. Wells calls it the Wandering Sickness, rather than atomic fallout. Most of the world then comes under the rule of fascist dictators, until 'the men of knowledge and the technicians'—I'm quoting from Wells's preface to the script—'and more particularly the aviators and transport engineers . . . take control and build up a new civilization on rational lines. This time it is a World Pax they create, for the political limitations of our present time have been washed out by forty years of confusion.' Confusion has never seemed to be an outstanding attribute of fascist dictators but, in any event, those forty years take us to 1976, only eight years ago, when World Peace was at last attained. O brave new world!

Van Doren and I agreed in 1935 that *Things to Come* was unsatisfactory as drama because the characters existed not as people but merely as mouthpieces for Wellsian rhetoric. Nor did we take it seriously as prophecy, but what I shall always remember is Van Doren's remark as we left the theatre: 'This film makes me realize that the future will never be futuristic. It will, of course, be like the present, only more so.'

My second futuristic experience took place a few years before I succeeded in finding a job with a publishing house. Shortly after I left college I worked as a minor employee at the Columbia Broadcasting System, where I met a brilliant executive, the late Paul Kesten, who was known around CBS as 'the vice president in charge of the future.' In the year 1939, he was responsible for what I believe to be the first television broadcast in New York. It was called 'Closed Circuit' because only a handful of TV sets then existed. They were owned by the network executives, who were greatly worried about this new invention. What effect was it going to have on their very successful radio business? What approach should they take to this new industry looming in the future? Paul Kesten had already made his decision. He knew RCA and NBC were working in black-and-white television, so he concluded that CBS should start with color, on the principle that people were quite used to Technicolor at the movies and would therefore favor color in the first TV sets.

Being a curious young man, I volunteered as an unpaid propman for 'Closed Circuit.' It was a one-hour vaudeville show, filmed in a big loft over the Grand Central Station, and featured a pair of ballet dancers in a *pas de deux*, a magician with a wand and a hatful of tricks, an old-fashioned one-act play called 'The Monkey's Paw,' and so on. Apparently CBS put a great deal of time and money into these trial runs as well as into their color

TV sets and cameras, but when television exploded into a national craze after the war, it was RCA's inexpensive black-and-white sets that prevailed. The novelty was so great that the public never noticed the absence of color, and Paul Kesten's shrewd prognostication was wrong by decades.

Timing was also the operative factor in my third experience with the misinterpretation or mistaking of the mythic future. This time it involved a book, George Orwell's *Nineteen Eighty-Four*, one of the most interesting and famous books I've ever worked on as an editor. While we were putting it through the press in 1949, I exchanged letters with the author and the English publisher, Frederick Warburg, and I can only say that the many articles, TV programs, editorials, and essays inspired by the actual arrival of 1984 have almost all missed the point. With two notable exceptions— Anthony Burgess and Mary Lee Settle—no writer seems to have perceived that Orwell's book was dealing not with the Future but the Present. Though it was published in 1949, Orwell wrote it in 1948, intending to call it *The Last Man in Europe*, but when he finished, he felt it needed a better title and invented a very good one by reversing the last two digits of 1948. As Anthony Burgess has said, the novel is 'less a prophecy' than 'an image of England as it was in the immediate postwar era, a land of gloom and shortages,' combined with 'the bizarrely impossible notion of British intellectuals taking over the government of the country.' Mary Lee Settle, the distinguished novelist and author of the *Beulah Quintet*, has shown in detail that the book is a picture of the Cold War period of 1948, when Newspeak and Doublethink were already operative, as Orwell's essays had long been predicting and as *Animal Farm*'s slogan, 'All animals are equal, but some are more equal than others,' brilliantly demonstrated. (Incidentally, in 1946 I was scolded by another publisher for publishing *Animal Farm*. He said he had turned it down because, after all, Russia had been our ally, which prompted me to say, 'Do you see it as a book about Russia? I thought it was all about pigs.') Mary Lee Settle has pointed out that the use of the threat of torture by rats, which breaks Winston Smith's resistance, comes out of *Homage to Catalonia*, Orwell's earlier book about the Spanish war, in which he describes his horror at seeing so many rats in the trenches. She also cites Smith's conversation in the cafeteria with the philologist Syme, the Newspeak specialist, as a parody of the Wittgensteinian lingo so popular in England, especially at Cambridge, in 1948. Anthony Burgess has summed up the greatness of Orwell's novel in these words: 'The memorable residue of *Nineteen Eighty-Four* is the fact of the tenuousness of human freedom, the vulnerability of the human will, and the genuine power of applied science.'

The genuine power of applied science! These words take us immediately to the heart of the problem of the future of the book.

What effect will the electronics revolution and the new communications technology have on the book? They have already begun to bring change, and are bound to bring more change, yet I see these developments not as a threat but an opportunity for book publishing. For example, it is quite possible that books in the future may be produced as bubble-wrapped packages containing an electronic chip, a so-called 'mini-marvel' silicon flake, from which the purchaser can obtain a screen projection on his personal computer. Of course, the plastic bubble will have to include a dust jacket, identifying the book's title and contents, probably in the form of a printed card. I would certainly feel personal regret at the replacement of traditional books and would hope that the production of well-designed and well-printed books will continue as an art for those readers who, in spite of the new technology, will always want them. The purely aesthetic and tactile pleasure of holding a well-made book is one that many of us will never relinquish. The advent of the electronic-circuitry chip method of production would, it seems to me, pose a greater threat to the traditional printer than to the book publisher, for this method will introduce—the phrase is already in circulation—publishing without paper.

Some people are not aware that most publishers do not have printing plants of their own and must farm out the work of book production. But if publishers decide that electronics can produce books more economically than present methods, the new technology will inevitably—if not necessarily *universally*—prevail. The function of the book publisher is often hard to define, and I'm fond of repeating the experience of my friend, George Brockway, head of W. W. Norton, when he went to China. When the Chinese learned that he was an American book publisher, they asked him if he printed books. When he said no, they asked if he ran bookstores.

When he said no, they asked what did he do. When he said he *underwrote* books, they smiled politely but failed to comprehend.

There are, of course, many other modes of electronic publishing looming in the near future, if they have not already arrived—computer data bases, video casettes, video disks, direct broadcasting satellites, flat portable TV screens, floppy disks, and remote printing. This last method may relieve the publisher of having to guess at his print run in advance. He will be able to print copies to order—large quantities for jobbers and institutions, small quantities for individuals.

In my view the electronic media, including television, are not the enemy of books. If to some extent they are competitors, they can also be a stimulus to book sales. Think of Scribner's experience with John Galsworthy's *The Forsythe Saga*, when it appeared on public television. This group of novels, so popular in the 1920s, had practically sunk out of sight when the well-produced dramatic series revived Galsworthy all over again as a best seller. Viking Penguin had the same experience, after so many years, with Robert Graves's *I, Claudius*. Television dramatizations even of classic novels, like *Anna Karenina* or Balzac, can create a new demand and a new audience for an old book. Apparently viewers who have never read such a book find the characters and story so vivid and interesting that they want to preserve the experience in the more permanent form of a book. Even though they have seen the dramatization, some viewers want to relive it again, or, one might say, possess it, by owning the book. Reading allows a slower pace and provides verbal subtleties and pleasures that are beyond the powers of the necessarily simplified visual version. Good television is definitely a stimulus to the reading of books.

Will the new forms that books take in the age of electronics attract or appeal to readers? A text projected on, or printed by, a computer would either appear on a screen—an unpleasant way to read, though we've been doing it in libraries for years with microfilms!—or as a print-out, probably on a folded-over continuous sheet. In the latter form, the reader would be provided not with a conventional book but a pile of paper. Is this so very different from the authors' typescripts I receive every day? It's important to remember how quickly the novelty of technology wears off.

One recalls the various metamorphoses of the telephone, which actually frightened some people on its introduction in the nineteenth century. Now we think nothing of walking from one room to another, or outdoors, with a cordless phone or of carrying some form of telephone wherever we may go. As for the typewriter in one of its newest forms, the word processor, I recently asked three well-known writers I happened to be lunching with whether they had any knowledge of or opinion about this new invention. To my surprise, Robert Fitzgerald, professor of rhetoric and oratory emeritus at Harvard, said he had completed his translation of the last two books of *The Aenead* (a superb translation, by the way) on a word processor. It saved him days and hours of tedious work. Aileen Ward, author of the best biography of John Keats, told me she owned a *portable* word processor, which she takes everywhere. She finds it so helpful it would now be hard for her to work without it. I agreed with the third writer, Professor Richard Sewall of Yale, author of the definitive biography of Emily Dickinson, who admitted that he had never seen or used a word processor, that we had both better look into it.

Not only does the novelty of technology quickly wear off, but in no way does it alter the fundamental nature of creative writing, which will always be subjective. The Greek word for writer means 'maker,' the word Igor Stravinsky preferred to composer or musician. Writers are makers, and they will inevitably use whatever tool or tools that may come to hand, from quill pens to word processors. What really interests me, as an editor and publisher, and what must be of the most serious concern to authors, is *what are the words on the electronic chip?* Are they well expressed? Are they worth reading? When we talk about the future of the book, we really mean the future of literature—at least I do.

The information that can be stored in data banks is enormous and useful. It is both the product of, and a quantum contribution to, the knowledge explosion of this century. It is with the distribution of this kind of information, rather than literature, that electronic publishing is predominantly concerned. A whole new vocabulary is already being introduced into our language—words and phrases like information float, software systems, image digitizers, high-speed data networking, distributed processing, algorithms, structured design and techniques, imaging system designs, digital signal processing, microprocessor-based real-time controllers—one of my favorites—servo loops for motion control, and, of course, computer graphics. We've all seen the full-page ads for workshop courses in computer graphics, announcing that 'We're heading for the Twenty-first Century' (how true), as well as the Xerox Company ads soliciting engineers to become pioneers in the transformation from paper to nonpaper electronic publishing. The fact is that we are well into the electronics era. I feel no alarm, or even disquiet, about this. For most of this century, we have been living in a technological age.

What I care about, and what I have tried to publish all my life, is literature. Poetry, fiction, biography, drama, history, philosophy—they can all make use of technology. Why not? Like data banks, they might even become *sources* of information because of their creative nature. They are *beyond* machines in the sense that their creation is subjective and personal. Western literature begins with Homer, and we know from the *Iliad* that human nature in ancient times is exactly like human nature in modern times. A great soldier gets angry and sulks and foolishly harms himself and others; a group of old men sitting on the city wall can't help marveling at the sight of a beautiful woman—the cause of the war—as she approaches them at the tower gates; an old king comes humbly in the night to beg for the body of his dead son. These are images and events we have known for centuries through one of our earliest books. As yesterday's symposium proved, the book has been with us a very long time. One of the earliest references to book publishing occurs in the Bible (a word which itself means book or books). Near the end of Ecclesiastes, the Preacher (who is said to date from the fifth century B.C. and whose memorable refrain is 'Vanity of vanities, all is vanity') says, 'Of the making of *many* books there is no end.'

If the Bible is on my mind, it is owing to an experience I had only a few weeks ago. I was in the Sinai desert, at one of the oldest monasteries in the world, St. Catherine's, which houses one of the oldest continuous libraries in the world and was the original home of the Codex Sinaiticus, the oldest biblical text (now in the British Library). St. Catherine's basilica, maintained by Greek Orthodox monks, was erected in the fifth century A.D. by the Emperor Justinian to mark the sacred spot on Mount

Horeb where Moses saw the burning bush and received the Law. As visitors, we were told that no one could enter the chapel of the burning bush, built over the roots of the original plant, which was located at the back of the basilica. But when we walked along the dirt path behind the edifice, we could see that the roots have thrust themselves out of the earth, and have climbed up the wall that surrounds the monastery. There, basking in the sun, we saw the blazing red raspberry bush. The guide told us that it grows only at this site; attempts to transplant it nearby have failed. As I looked at the burning bush, I thought: What a marvelous symbol of creativity! It cannot be kept down, it *will* blaze forth.

This experience makes me want to close with a toast: 'To the human spirit, may it always—no matter what technology may surround it—continue to insist on blazing forth in books.'

The Future of the Book

JAMES THORPE

For some time now, houses built by developers have rarely included book-shelves. The buyer is, however, always free to install a wall unit wherever he can manage it. The wall unit can provide space for books and other printed material along with space for electronic gear. That wall unit is, I think, a useful emblem for us to keep in mind. It is flexibly responsive to our needs and wishes. It can be given over mostly to books or mostly to electronics. It has now (let us suppose) a fair number of books in it. What will it be like in the future? Will it still have a fair number of books in it? Or more? Or less? Or none?

Another emblem for us. An image of a group of monks, in the scriptorium of their monastery, in the year 1484—half a millennium ago—discussing the Future of the Manuscript. Dare we suppose that they were about as bright as we are? Dare we suppose that they knew about as much about the future as we do? Dare we face the limits on our own ability to predict or control the future?

Two emblems presiding over us, working for us. The wall unit, with its changing mix of books and electronics. The monks in the scriptorium, the prototypes for our discussions.

My appointed task is to open up the question of the future of the book so far as scholars and libraries are concerned. What are the right questions to ask? They have to do, I suppose, with three matters. First:

What, in fact, are the real and continuing advantages of the book? Second: What are the main disadvantages of the book, so far as libraries are concerned? And third: What changes are likely in the patterns of human behavior that will affect the future of the book? Three questions. I wish I knew the answers. Here's a start.

The real advantages of the book. Go back to the beginnings. When printing from movable type first began, it conferred certain tremendous advantages on the book over the then current methods of disseminating texts. It could replicate text and illustrations quickly, at relatively low cost, and in essentially unlimited numbers. These advantages made the printed book heavily responsible for the intellectual and cultural and social revolutions of the last five hundred years. These central advantages are, of course, no longer unique to the printed book. On the other hand, the book does have some notable advantages.

First, the book can be portable and convenient to use under almost any circumstances. It can be designed and produced in almost any size or shape, for the vest pocket or coffee table, for the plane or space cruiser, for reading in bed or in another galaxy.

Second, it can be beautiful. Beautiful in its design, in its type and printing, in its illustrations, in its paper and binding and dust wrapper. It can, in fact, be an art object. The Grolier Club has made, throughout its history, important contributions to this ideal of the book. I regret to say that beauty does not now seem a very high priority for most publishers. Mostly, publishers try to cut production costs to keep the price of their books from becoming even more outrageous than they are. But I learned, many years ago, from a good book designer that most of the elements of the beauty of the book depend on taste, not money. And it is certainly possible to spend an apparently unlimited amount on production—as in the case of many corporate annual reports—and still have a really ugly book as the product.

Third, the book is relatively easy to consult. You can flip through it, skim it, stop at the parts of interest for a moment or for as long as you want to, check things from the index, see whether you want to spend time on that particular book. The book is especially handy if you don't know quite what you're looking for: if your ideas are in a state of flux, for example, and you don't even know what material will be of interest to you. This is a situation that most scholars I know have been in at one time or another, and some of us quite frequently. To be able to play with a lot of books is often the greatest possible aid to clarifying your own mind and setting you forth on your own independent course of thought.

Fourth, the book requires active intellectual involvement on the part of the reader. (I'm placing the book, here, in comparison with texts that come to us through the ear or as mainly pictorial representation.) To some people, this may not seem to be much of an advantage, as we do not always prefer the active intellectual involvement of reading a book. But it is an advantage in the sense that our response is richer and deeper to the degree that we are more involved in the process of communication. In fact, when we read a book, we have to perform the text, whether our reading is aloud or silent. And our effort to perform it—the expressiveness we give to the text—makes us try harder to come to terms with it.

A fifth advantage of the book has to do with its symbolic status and its sense of permanence. It has long been held in respect as a significant object that preserves our cultural heritage. A work published on microfilm or microfiche, for example, never seems to be quite published, no matter how many thousands of copies may be distributed throughout the world. (Moreover, in the academic world, deans and promotion committees don't take such pseudo-books as real 'contributions to knowledge.') The book itself is solid and real, like the stone that Dr. Johnson kicked to disprove Bishop Berkeley. At least you can't easily erase it—and certainly not accidentally—and the book has proved to be a very difficult object to burn, even by the Inquisitors themselves.

The esteem for the book is partly associational and poetic, perhaps. Many of us are doubtless simply sentimental about books. Patterns of sentiment tend to outlive patterns of behavior, just as the fondness for Elizabethan thatched cottages was preserved long after no one would have chosen to live in one through a raw English winter if he had a better choice. The aura surrounding the book may fade away in due course, but it seems likely to stay with us for another few generations.

So here, tentatively, are some possible ways of thinking about advantages of the printed book as we know it. One or two of these advantages—

such as the portability advantage—will in due course be shared by other methods of communication, but maybe in a more limited way than the book offers. These advantages mainly benefit the users of books. Let me now say a word or two about certain disadvantages of books, offered from my announced perspective of libraries.

The most notable disadvantage of books is their cost, ranging from expensive to impossible. I include within this disadvantage current reference and scholarly books as well as rare books from the past. The main disadvantages of books so far as libraries are concerned are, in fact, almost all economic. Books are costly to buy, to service, and to keep in repair. They are bulky and take up a lot of expensive space, especially when we are talking about hundreds of thousands or millions of books in a single repository.

If an accurate cost analysis were made concerning the use of books in major libraries, the results would probably be staggering, especially since in a large, comprehensive library, the average books are very infrequently consulted. Setting aside popular texts and key reference books, a library book may be used once every few years, perhaps. At the Huntington Library, about thirty thousand rare books are consulted each year out of a collection of some 350,000 rare books; that works out to be almost twelve years elapsed time between consultations of the average rare book. But the value of a library to a specialized user is the fact that the book is there and available when it is needed, no matter how long that book has to languish between consultations.

For a century or so, it has been generally felt that every member of society has a natural right to the free use of the books that he or she wants or needs. This state of affairs was encouraged by the likes of Andrew Carnegie and supported (as a matter of social policy) at all levels of government, by colleges and universities and independent libraries and foundations, and by generous benefactors who were interested in books.

I believe that this state of affairs will be changing, probably within the next generation or two. Libraries are buying fewer books because their income has not increased as much as the cost of books. Moreover, the cost of book services has increased even more markedly than their purchase prices. I think that some of our largest libraries that are not integrated into universities are in real financial trouble and that others will be. I don't see any relief in sight for libraries; I think that the cost of books and services will probably continue to increase in real dollars. These matters have some bearing on the future of the book. As business managers assume greater responsibility for the fiscal operation of libraries, some reviews will doubtless lead to changes more radical than belt tightening.

Libraries are caught in the cross fire of the love of tradition and the desire to survive. Libraries are among our most conservative institutions, and the love of tradition urges their managers to keep providing the same service in the same way as before. Chains were taken off of the books only reluctantly.

But the desire to survive urges the managers of libraries to find new ways of providing a similar service more inexpensively and (preferably) better. Much has happened in this century, with the use of microforms, of quick copying, of central cataloguing, of computer networks joining libraries to a central data base (OCLC and RLIN), and the like.

Much more stands on the horizon. I can see a complete national (or international) union catalogue of printed books in computer storage, and a similar catalogue of manuscripts, with full access to all of the data from terminals at participating libraries.

I can imagine many libraries giving up collecting certain classes of books: light entertainment, for example, or other types of books that could made available to consumers at their local supermarket on cassettes or microchips; or books that consist essentially of factual information that can be stored as data for ready retrieval; or books that are highly specialized in nature, for which the predicted long-range frequency of consultation might be no more than once in five years to begin with, and less later. I can imagine libraries making an effort to phase out books in any collecting areas for which some reasonably satisfactory alternative can be found. If some of these changes were to take place, they might well lead publishers to alter the form of publication of some of their products from printed books to an electronic form for on-demand publishing, on-line use, or personal computer use through disks or chips. These may be the books of the future, but the future of the book is a larger question, including (as it must) all the books of the past and the continuing tradition of the printed book, perhaps in a more limited form. These imaginings are, I think, not very far-fetched. Indeed, I believe that these matters—or something like them—are very likely to happen in this country in the relatively near future.

I have frequently heard the fear expressed that we are headed for a split in our culture. On the one hand, there will be high culture—what we have recognized from the past as poetry, fiction, art, music, drama, and so forth, typified by what we call 'the good book.' And on the other hand will be what is termed pop culture—the whole world of situation comedies, newscasters, professional sports, rock concerts, popular records and tapes, and all the rest of our entertainment that has a mass audience.

I don't like elitism, either, and it is a little embarrassing to feel out of step with your own world. But I think that the split in our culture is already here—indeed, that it has always been here. It seems to me that every culture has always offered a wide range of alternatives for different tastes and needs. One wants to see people truly attracted to the artistic and cultural manifestations that will enrich their experience most fully and prove most rewarding to them. Some have always wished people to be better educated and more cultivated and to appreciate a 'higher' culture than they do, but that has never rejoined the split. What is different about the split now is, first, that it is quite sharp and, second, that we have the technical means to satisfy the needs of pop culture very much more easily than we can satisfy the needs of high culture. Pop culture is flourishing mightily, and high culture is at risk.

I have mentioned a few details of possible changes in library collections. I can also imagine the possibility of some corollary changes in the character of many libraries. A change away from libraries as intellectual and cultural and learning centers. A change in the direction of libraries as information centers. If these changes were to come to pass, they could make a profound difference in the future of the book.

More important, such changes would be another decisive move away from a human-centered world. We have already accepted the idea of current decades as the Information Revolution and the move toward an information-centered world, without quite realizing that we will be giving up a great deal of human value to the process.

For a final imagining, I expect that it will be technically possible, ultimately, to have full access to the text of all the books and manuscripts themselves from terminals at convenient locations. With something even approaching that state, there would be no need for more than a few major repositories, and much less need for the future publication of printed books in the sense that we know them. I think that this state won't be reached within the next few decades, in part because it may be thought too expensive to set up, and in part because a lot of objections may arise from those who use and like books. And I think it will certainly not drive the printed book from the scene.

I have been talking about the future of the book from the library perspective. Economic considerations have weighed heavily in these thoughts, and I have gaily supposed that the electronic alternatives to the printed book that are already available will be economically feasible—and that other alternatives will be invented—more quickly than most of us are willing to suppose.

Let me take one final tack and talk about the behavioral bases for the future of the book. A fundamental way of thinking about the future of the book is to speculate on the value changes that seem likely in our society. We have been urged to feel absolutely free to speculate as to what the future holds in store for the book. So here are some thoughts for possible discussion, if they interest you.

My underlying proposition is that human behavior is guided by the controlling values that one acknowledges as governing one's society, and that those accepted values change slowly over a period of time as new circumstances present themselves. Many values are relevant, in one way or another, to the book and to its future. The obvious one is the way we value the word, the degree to which we are word-oriented. But there are many other values that also deserve consideration. The value we place on numbers, our number-orientation. And our image-orientation. And our sound-orientation. I would like to speak a little about each of these human orientations in terms of the value that is placed on it within Western society. Where we are now. What value changes seem likely. And how any changes will affect the future of the book.

To begin with, our word-orientation. The word has long been associated with our highest intellectual values. We have esteem for persons who are comfortable with words, special esteem for those who are quick with words. Those who understand words with ease and handle them with fluency are regarded as highly intelligent, and they get the top rankings in most of our ordering systems. If you are good in some other expressive mode—such as painting pictures—the world may rate you high as a painter, but it will not necessarily believe that you are highly intelligent, as it would if you were a dealer in words. The word possesses something like magic for us: when Beowulf unlocks his word-hoard, school is out for Grendel, and for Grendel's dam. The word also has for us a touch of divinity in it, through the Greek *logos* and the conversion of scripture to the Word—from writings to the Word—by evangelical speakers.

Western society has been principally word-oriented—so far as intellectual and cultural matters are concerned—for a couple of thousand years. My guess is that this orientation will be seen as having reached its peak in the eighteenth and nineteenth centuries, and that it is now giving ground, and that its place in the value system will gradually decline during the foreseeable future.

The great increase in our number-orientation got underway two or three centuries ago. In our own century, however, its place in our value system has risen spectacularly. Science, business, government, finance, and the social sciences have assumed larger and more important places in our lives, and their method of thinking and of communicating is more and more dependent on numbers. I believe that it will rise much higher in our value system than it is now. Number-orientation becomes increasingly important as society becomes larger in size and more complex in nature. I see an ever-increasing number-orientation for the foreseeable future.

I will speak of our image-orientation and our sound-orientation together. They are not intrinsically related, but their progress has been similar. Images (in the form of pictures and visual representations and depictions of all sorts) and sound (typically music) have always had an important but secondary place in Western society. Now, in this century, they are moving nearer to the center of our cultural consciousness, thanks to the developments in photography, film, television, sound reproduction systems, and a multitude of electronic devices. Image and sound are now the great transmitters of popular culture, and they have both the high esteem of their consumers and the disesteem of those who feel superior to popular culture.

My guess is that the orientation to image and sound will become more and more central to our cultural and intellectual experience, that gradually they will gain in the esteem of the self-selected body of our intellectual leaders, and that gradually we will achieve a much more sophisticated perception of image and sound, which I think we now understand rather crudely.

In short, I think that the value changes within the next century will all tend to reduce the paramount position of the word. Since the book as we know it depends mainly on communication by words, this argument suggests that the book will be less central to our intellectual and cultural life than it has been. Less central and less dominant, but still crucially important to the world of culture and the world of learning.

And what of our emblems, the wall unit and the monks? The wall unit looks as if it will have somewhat fewer books in it, but they will be of prime value. And the monks? Like us, they look bemused.

An Introduction to the New Literacy

BENJAMIN M. COMPAINE

Literacy itself has never been a static concept. Over centuries, the bundle of skills we call literacy has evolved with technology, as well as with the political, economic, and social systems. The current notion of literacy has evolved from the technology of the quill pen, paper, movable type, and the mechanically powered rotary press.

The New Literacy is the skills that may be required to function in society and the thought processes[1] that may evolve as the result of the current and future changes in the methods by which information is stored, manipulated, and transmitted. Increasingly, information is being digitally stored in some electronic medium and being delivered to users by telecommunications or via devices that can make the information readable, viewable, or audible. The continuation of these trends will, over time, create the need for a new bundle of skills and processes that will define the New Literacy.

The foundation of a New Literacy is the cultural change that is likely to come about from the increased use of digital electronic processes. There is basis in history for it. There is circumstantial evidence in the present

---

1. 'Process' as it is associated with 'thinking' or 'thought' process is used here to mean the mental algorithms that are *learned* by members of different cultures. It is not a reference to physiological paths in the brain that enable and control thought.

that the consequences of a possible change in the fundamentals of literacy need to be taken seriously. Historian Elizabeth Eisenstein, in considering the impact of printing on Western civilization, noted that while it is relatively easy to describe the development of printing in the fifteenth century, 'It is another thing to decide how access to a greater abundance or variety of written records affected ways of learning, thinking, and perceiving among literate elites.'[2]

The key issues in the notion of a New Literacy are in seeking some understanding of the influence of modern information technologies on ways of learning, thinking, and perceiving, not only by literate elites but by the general public as well.

TRADITIONAL LITERACY · History provides a wealth of precedents for the changes we are experiencing today. Each generation seems to think its problems or opportunities are unique. History sometimes shows us quite the opposite. The development of low-cost computer power and its attendant implications for educational, industrial, social, and political structures all have antecedents. For example, the introduction of photography in the nineteenth century collided with the popular wisdom about the role of art and painting. Then, the questions were about the new technology of the photographic process and how it might affect human views on the reality of war or on creativity. Today, similar types of questions are being raised about the effect electronic publishing is having on print and about the impact of television and video games on children.

The development of current notions of literacy is closely tied to the technologies of the printing press and the steam engine. An understanding of the previous evolution in technology and literacy is context for today's changes.

WHAT IS LITERACY? · Literacy frequently describes a range of skills. It is used to mean the ability to read and write in one's vernacular. Being 'literate' may mean being familiar with the great works of literature and philosophy of a culture. Sometimes it is also applied to basic skills, such as

2. Elizabeth L. Eisenstein, *The Printing Press as An Agent of Change* (Cambridge, England and New York: Cambridge University Press, 1979), p. 8.

the ability to fill out a bank check properly or to understand simple written instructions. We also see the term literacy modified by very specific skills. A person who can identify the works of composers might be referred to as being musically literate. Today, the ability to write programs in computer languages that make the computers perform tasks is being called computer literacy. Indeed, the mastery of almost any skill can be called a literacy. The term literacy itself comes from the Latin *litteratus*, or marked with letters. In medieval usage, to be literate meant to be learned in Latin, not simply the ability to read and write in the vernacular.

Today, I am not describing merely a narrow meaning such as computer literacy, or the ability to program a computer or work a computer for its own intrinsic worth. As a starting point, this paper accepts a point of view that literacy in modern Western society is 'a complex cultural phenomenon involving relations between attitudes towards language and mechanical skills.'[3] The attitudes involve a consciousness of the uses and problems of language, this awareness being the foundation of literacy. But the pragmatic aspect of a literacy is the means by which this consciousness is expressed. Twentieth-century American culture holds that the skills of being able to read and write are at the foundation of literacy.

This has not always been the case, however. Before the written record came into widespread use in eleventh-century England, the oral tradition predominated. To be literate meant the ability to compose and recite orally—in Latin, of course. Into the twelfth century, to make a record of something meant to bear oral witness, not to produce a document for others to read. Even where written records existed, 'the spoken word was the legally valid record.'[4]

Moreover, because of the difficulty of writing with a quill on parchment or with a stylus on wax, writing was considered a special skill that 'was not automatically coupled with the ability to read.'[5] The most common way of committing words to writing in twelfth-century England was by dictating to a scribe, who was a craftsman and not necessarily himself

---

3. Robert Pattison, *On Literacy* (New York: Oxford University Press, 1982), p. 118.
4. M. T. Clanchy, *From Memory to Written Record: England, 1066–1307* (Cambridge, Mass.: Harvard University Press, 1979), p. 56.
5. Ibid., p. 88.

able to compose. Thus, reading and dictating were typically paired, rather than reading and writing.

Reading and writing are the basic skills. In nineteenth-century England, the goal of bringing reading and writing skills to the common man was not an end in itself. According to the literati, it was not merely the ability to read but the reading of the 'right' material that separated the truly literate from the great unwashed. The printed word was supposed to bring spiritual enrichment and intellectual enlightenment to the English nation. Novel reading was held in particularly low esteem by some elements of the literati, with much the same disdain held today by some sectors of society for commercial television, video games, and even the multitude of self-help and how-to books. In 1879, an English librarian told a meeting that 'schoolboys or students who took to novel reading to any great extent never made much progress in after life.'[6] The irony of this should not be lost on those who are convinced that television and even newer electronic media are eroding literacy. What they really mean is that they menace the *traditional* concept of literacy.

WRITING, PRINTING, AND LINEAR THINKING · History provides the strongest argument at this time that if a new literacy emerges from the expanding use of computers and telecommunications it will have a profound—if unpredictable—impact on society. The fundamental impact of written compared to oral literacy cultures on thought processes has been the grist for philosophers, sociologists, anthropologists, psychologists, historians, and linguists for thousands of years. Socrates told the story of the reaction of Thamus, king of Egypt, when he was introduced to the art of writing: '. . . [T]his invention [writing],' said Thamus, 'will produce forgetfulness in the souls of those who have learned it. They will not need to exercise their memories, being able to rely on what is written, calling things to mind no longer from within themselves, . . . but under the stimulus of external marks. . . .'[7]

6. Richard D. Altick, *The English Common Reader: A Social History of the Mass Reading Public 1800–1900* (Chicago: University of Chicago Press, 1974), p. 233.

7. W. C. Helmhold and W. G. Rabinowitz, trans., *Plato's Phaedrus* (New York: The Liberal Arts Press, 1956), p. 68.

Thus, the notion that writing fosters a thought process different from a verbal literacy is an old one. Goody, Innis, McLuhan, and Ong, among others, address the relationship between thought processes and the technology of expression. In general, this group of writers proposes that the development of alphabets consisting of a small number of symbols made possible 'a stage of logical thinking that is not possible in cultures with only an oral tradition.'[8]

Symbols, such as letters, words, and numbers, are used to convey information. Education to a large extent is the process of teaching children to master the manipulation of the symbols used in a given culture. Writing made possible the development of logic and specialized learning. The relationship between writing and rational thinking is central to the notion of the New Literacy because the power of digital information processes has the potential to restructure the way in which we use writing.

There is an abundance of indicators that suggests that writing, and by derivation, printing, has helped develop a logical, sequential—hence linear—thought process in modern literate societies. Ideas of cause and effect are in the form of things in sequence, a relationship that some anthropologists, linguists, and others believe is alien to predominantly oral cultures. David Hume argued in the eighteenth century that there is no causality indicated in any sequence, yet in Western literate society we adhere to the notion that certain things must follow from others.

The traditional linear literacy, therefore, is tied to writing and to print, to sequential thought, to logic, and to rational notions of cause and effect.

OTHER CONSEQUENCES OF CHANGE TO WRITTEN LITERACY · Print, of course, did not burst upon Europe in the fifteenth century and suddenly change what had been a predominantly oral culture. Indeed, the oral tradition did not and has not died. When men learn to write they do not forget how to speak.

The gradual emergence of written texts and then printing in medieval England, and with them the rise of reading and writing skills, did, of

8. Daniel P. Resnick, "Spreading the Word: An Introduction," *Literacy*, p. 3.

course, have consequences. These included new kinds of social structures, such as bureaucracy and business, that were encouraged by reading and writing skills.

PLAYERS AND STAKES · The notion of a New Literacy has implications that could permeate all aspects of society and institutions. Some constituencies are affected directly. Print media businesses are asking about the future of their ink-on-paper products. Should they take comfort in the current resistance of the mass consumer to switch to electronically delivered information services, or will the next generation of potential newspaper/ magazine/book buyers be more responsive to electronic retrieval and manipulation? Banks and other financial institutions have already found a sizable segment of customers (initially their younger ones) ready to use automatic teller machines. Now, in Great Britain, a relatively small savings bank has made the strategic decision to channel capital funds into providing customers with video terminals for electronic home banking instead of building branch offices. Will similar decisions start to be made on a similar scale elsewhere in the industrialized world?

Educators are among the most concerned about immediate implications, in particular on issues of curriculum design and materials budgets. Questions are being raised about what schools and centers of higher education should be teaching. Spelling? Arithmetic? Business institutions ranging from smokestack industries to high-tech research organizations are trying to predict their need for certain skills. They are looking for answers to concerns about productivity and product or service quality. Government policymakers are involved with direct questions, such as priorities for expenditures for education and job retraining, and indirect issues, as seen in international trade concerns and the desirability of an agenda for a national industrial policy.

The stakes involved in the New Literacy are immense, although not all quantifiable. If the education community is slow to understand and respond to changes, the loss will not be in terms of jobs for teachers or in sales of textbooks, but in *long-term* effects on society and, in the case of a given state or locality, the ability of its industry to compete with others who were more responsive. The failure of a newspaper publishing company to recognize the coming of a New Literacy may result in an erosion of its traditional business and, perhaps, loss of market opportunity for new business. Nevertheless, neither type of change is likely to happen overnight. For many years, there may be little hard evidence of fundamental shifts resulting from the skills incorporated into literacy. Then, the confluence of several needed technological developments and the maturing of cultural trends may result in relatively rapid effects.

For example, one frequently expressed technology-based reason given for why electronic display will not replace print is the relative crudeness of the resolution of video displays compared to printed text. Reading text from a screen for extended periods has been blamed for headaches and eye stress. Full screen video displays are also not portable and are thus considered at a disadvantage compared to print. Similarly, a typical culturally based apology for print is provided by a group that is funded by the book industry: '. . . [I]n the public consciousness books lend permanence, respectability, and credibility to a venture. The popular image of the book—which some people had expected to be demolished by competition from the electronic and non-print media—remains unchallenged as a symbol of knowledge.'[9]

However, recent experience with electronics in general, and with semiconductor technology in particular, suggests that portable, high-resolution flat screens are in the offing. Several manufacturers are already marketing portable television sets using liquid crystal flat screens. It is reasonable to assume that within the foreseeable future, the argument of portability and resolution will cease to be an issue. Similarly, work is proceeding with downloading text (that is, sending text via telephone, cable, or even broadcast to an electronic storage medium) or simply selling in retail stores complete works of print encoded in semiconductor modules. When, and at what cost, these developments will be ready for the mass market is less crucial for this discussion than is the point that technology is likely to provide the necessary infrastructure for a New Literacy.

9. John P. Dessauer, *Trends Update*, Book Industry Study Group (New York, August 1983), p. 2. Quotation attributed to John Huenefeld.

FORCES AND TRENDS SHAPING NEW LITERACY · Print was not so much a break with the past as it was a technological force that contributed to an already well-established trend started in England in the eleventh century: growing use of written records instead of records stored in human memory. Similarly, the current premise is that the effects of recent electronic technological developments in computers and communications are a continuation of a long and well-documented historical process. Video games, personal computers, compunications, the increasing cost of paper and physical delivery, widespread use of automatic teller machines, electronic mail, growth in electronic data base publishing, and others are not isolated nor mutually exclusive developments. They are pieces of a dynamic process in much the same tradition as were, for example, the development of the steam-driven rotary press, the spread of the railroads, innovation in manufacturing of cheap paper, and improvement in optics for eyeglasses.

Computers have been purchased by the millions for homes and schools, with prices of useable systems now under six hundred dollars and continuing to drop. Video games, which achieved sales of about eight billion dollars in 1982, are merging with home computers that can play the games as well as perform simple word processing, educational programs, household programs, and write-it-yourself programs.

In offices, the success of the IBM personal computer and other computers in the above-one-thousand-dollar category is largely due to the functions these machines have successfully performed, in particular the spread-sheet calculations, word processing, data base management, and information retrieval for small and medium businesses that previously could not afford computerized operations. Well over two million personal computers in the above-one-thousand-dollar category were shipped in 1983 alone. Large businesses are using the personal computers to place direct computer power at the hands of more people. Travelers Insurance Co., as one example, had two thousand PCs in its offices by 1983 and had formal arrangements for ten thousand more by 1986. Aetna Casualty and Life figured it had one video display terminal for each six employees in 1982 but expected to have one terminal per two workers by 1985.

There are at least fifteen million adults working with VDTs as part of

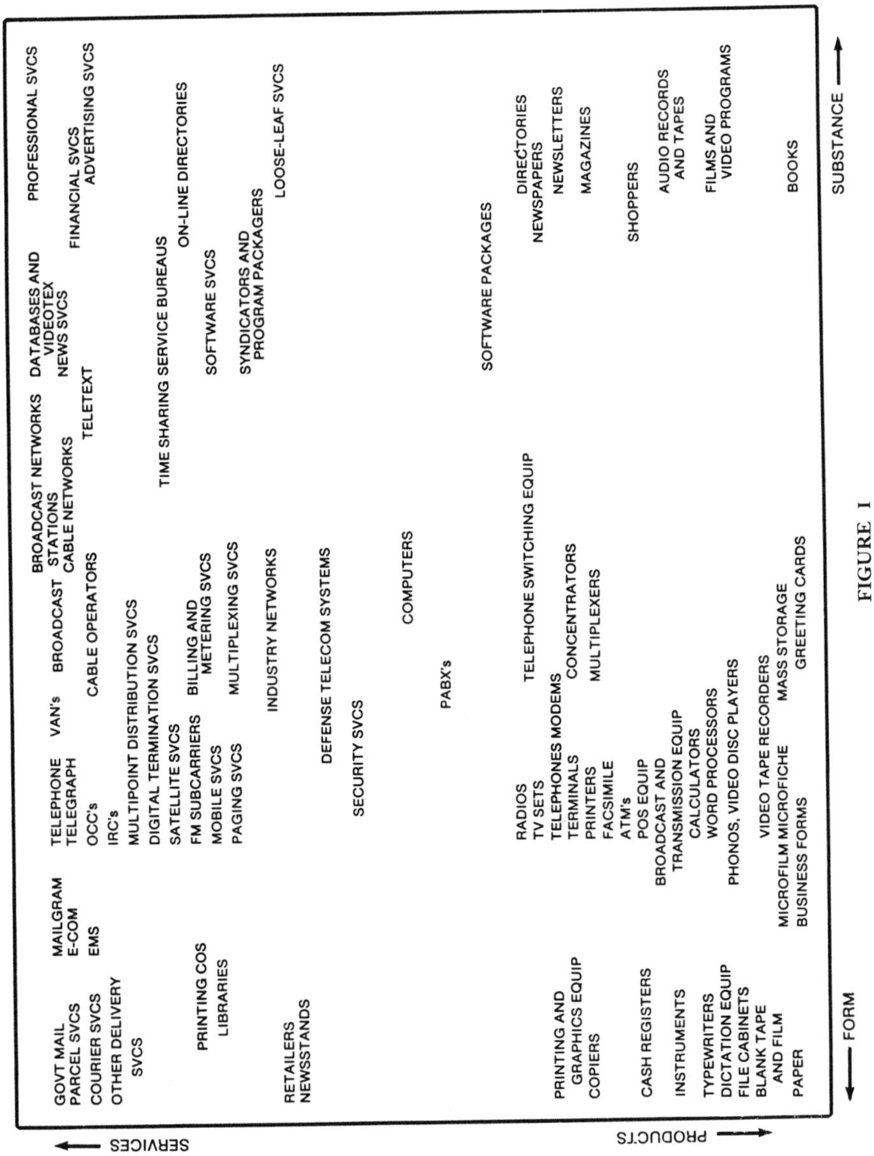

GOVT MAIL
PARCEL SVCS
COURIER SVCS
OTHER DELIVERY
SVCS

MAILGRAM
E-COM
EMS

TELEPHONE
TELEGRAPH

VAN's

BROADCAST
CABLE OPERATORS

BROADCAST NETWORKS
STATIONS
CABLE NETWORKS

TELETEXT

DATABASES AND
VIDEOTEX
NEWS SVCS

PROFESSIONAL SVCS

FINANCIAL SVCS
ADVERTISING SVCS

OCC's
IRC's
MULTIPOINT DISTRIBUTION SVCS
DIGITAL TERMINATION SVCS

TIME SHARING SERVICE BUREAUS

ON-LINE DIRECTORIES

PRINTING COS

LIBRARIES

SATELLITE SVCS
FM SUBCARRIERS
MOBILE SVCS
PAGING SVCS

BILLING AND
METERING SVCS

MULTIPLEXING SVCS

SOFTWARE SVCS

SYNDICATORS AND
PROGRAM PACKAGERS

LOOSE-LEAF SVCS

RETAILERS
NEWSSTANDS

INDUSTRY NETWORKS

DEFENSE TELECOM SYSTEMS

SECURITY SVCS

COMPUTERS

PABX's

SOFTWARE PACKAGES

DIRECTORIES
NEWSPAPERS
NEWSLETTERS
MAGAZINES

SHOPPERS

AUDIO RECORDS
AND TAPES

FILMS AND
VIDEO PROGRAMS

BOOKS

RADIOS
TV SETS
TELEPHONES MODEMS
TERMINALS
PRINTERS
FACSIMILE
ATM's
POS EQUIP

TELEPHONE SWITCHING EQUIP

CONCENTRATORS

MULTIPLEXERS

PRINTING AND
GRAPHICS EQUIP
COPIERS

CASH REGISTERS

BROADCAST AND
TRANSMISSION EQUIP

INSTRUMENTS

CALCULATORS
WORD PROCESSORS

TYPEWRITERS
DICTATION EQUIP
FILE CABINETS
BLANK TAPE
AND FILM
PAPER

PHONOS, VIDEO DISC PLAYERS

VIDEO TAPE RECORDERS

MICROFILM MICROFICHE
BUSINESS FORMS

MASS STORAGE

GREETING CARDS

← FORM

← SERVICES

← PRODUCTS →

SUBSTANCE →

FIGURE 1

THE 'INFORMATION BUSINESS'

© 1983 by President and Fellows of Harvard College

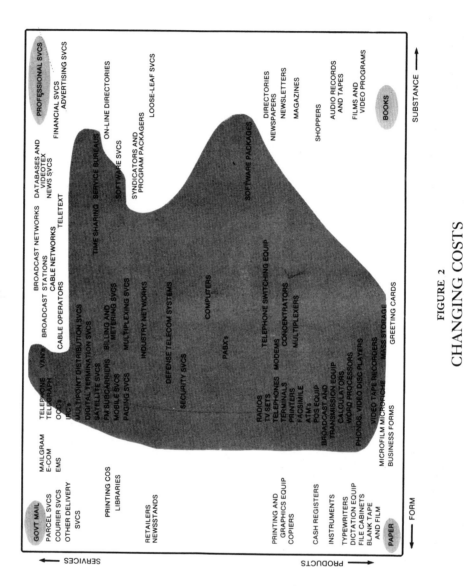

FIGURE 2

CHANGING COSTS

© 1984 Program on Information Resources Policy, Harvard University

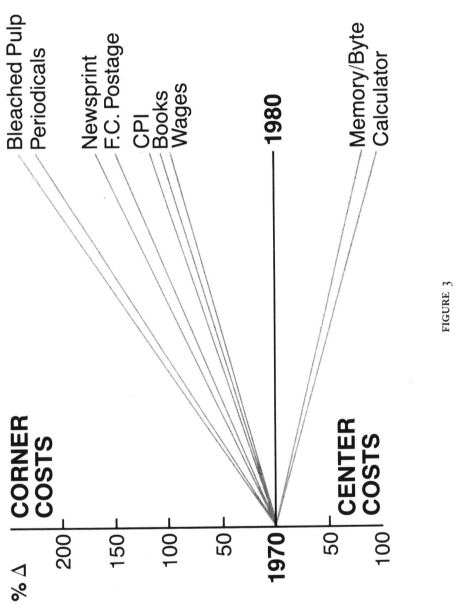

FIGURE 3

© 1984 Program on Information Resources Policy, Harvard University

81

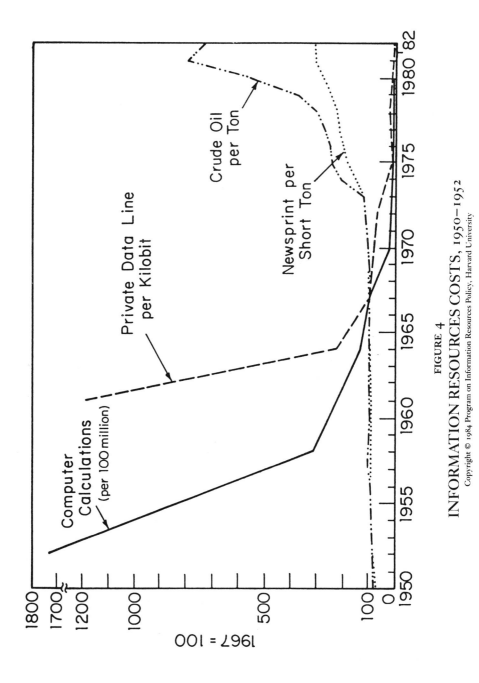

FIGURE 4

INFORMATION RESOURCES COSTS, 1950–1952

Copyright © 1984 Program on Information Resources Policy, Harvard University

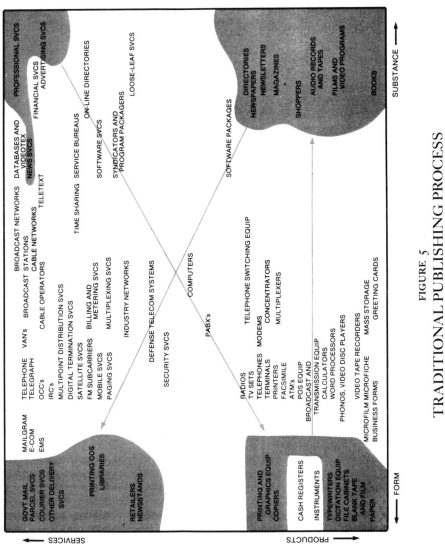

FIGURE 5

TRADITIONAL PUBLISHING PROCESS

© 1984 Program on Information Resources Policy, Harvard University

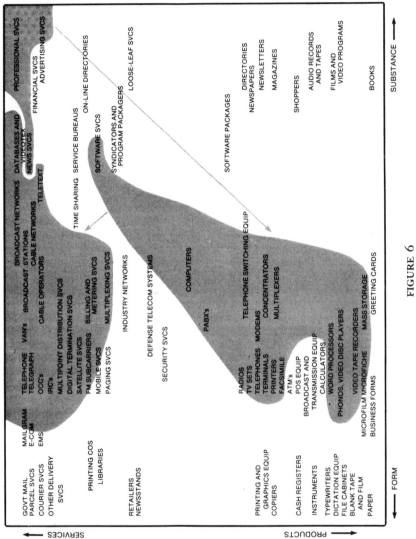

FIGURE 6

ELECTRONIC PUBLISHING PROCESS

© 1984 Program on Information Resources Policy, Harvard University

their daily routines.[10] They include secretaries using word processors; order-takers for catalogue retailers; reservation clerks at airlines, car rental agencies, and travel agencies; stockbrokers checking securities prices; newspaper reporters and editors creating tomorrow's edition; and lawyers researching court decisions. These are not necessarily the people being thought of when 'computer' literacy is discussed.

The notion that there is something special about 'the book' or about print is culturally derived. That is, we have become used to and comfortable with print. We have developed conventions for its use. 'Print' or 'video' are essentially examples of *formats* in which some content or substance can be displayed or otherwise manipulated by users. These are among a multitude of ways in which we can express information *substance*.

Process is the application of instruments, such as typewriters, computers, printing presses, the human brain, telephone wire, or delivery trucks in the creation, manipulation, storage, and transmission/distribution of substance in some intermediate or final format. For example, a traditional newspaper, an ink-on-paper format, relies on processes including entering thoughts of a reporter into a computer by manipulating a keyboard of a video display terminal with storage in the computer, the eventual creation of a printing plate, and distribution to consumers via trucks. Part of that process may be different should the same article be distributed to some consumers via a telephone link to a video display terminal. In that case, some of the process is the same (the entering and storing of information), the formats are different for the end user (text on screen versus ink on paper), but the substance may remain constant.

The message of the New Literacy is that changing processes and formats may have a long-term effect on how users deal with substance. A generation of children is being exposed to video games and computers at home and school. Unlike print, or even radio and television, these devices change the relationship between users and the process by which they receive information.

10. Personal conversation with Paul Strassmen, vice president, Xerox, 10 May 1984.

CONCLUSION · In summarizing a conference on electronic publishing in March 1984, John Dessauer wrote:

> The book printed on paper may not survive, though it will probably live on for yet a very long time because of its sublime simplicity and utility. What promises to survive permanently is the Written Word, if need be in new form. We must remember that books began their history as clay tablets, evolving later into papyrus rolls, with the medieval codex preceding the modern book, which was first designed by Aldus Manutius in 1501. If the book has already passed through several technological stages, it will probably continue doing so as new methods and improvements are developed. But when comprehensive analysis, intellectual perception, depth of understanding, keenness of vision, or profundity of grasp are sought, then the print medium in general and the book in particular are far better suited to provide them than are the computer or other electronic media.[11]

Although the direct causes and effects associated with literacy are controversial and unresolved, the ascendency of written over oral literacy in our society has had a profound impact on its development. The written record has encouraged a more sequential form of thinking. It has enabled us to define concepts with greater precision, to maintain archives and refer back to them for facts and definitions, and to weigh more deliberately the local and persuasive elements of issues. 'The capacity to employ various symbolized notations enables one to supplement one's memory, organize one's future activities, and communicate at one time with an indefinite number of individuals. . . .'

The interest in the potential confluence of forces that may be driving toward a fundamental change in the notion of literacy should not be confused with a prediction that it will indeed happen. Perhaps there is something inherent in print or in linear thought processes in man that will resist being upset by alternative ways of information acquisition and processing.

11. John P. Dessauer, "More about Books and Electronics," *Trends Update*, Book Industry Study Group (New York, April 1984), p. 2.

We have much to learn. But the weight of historical precedent would seem to come down in favor of being prepared for today's literate societies to acquire an expanded set of skills, tools, and processes for literacy. The consequences of this will have to remain just speculation.

The Museum Curator and Fine Prints:
Past, Present, and Future

ANDREW ROBISON

To indicate the approach to fine prints of a museum curator one hundred years ago, now, and in the future, I will begin with the past, specifically the past in Europe. At the time of the founding of The Grolier Club in 1884, there were already numerous public collections of prints, drawings, and illustrated books in Europe. Taking the founding of a separate department and the appointment of an official curator as a clear recognition of the distinct existence of a collection, the Bibliothèque Nationale's Cabinet des Estampes was founded in 1720; in 1884 it was under the direction of the Comte Henri Delaborde. The British Museum Print Room was founded in 1808 and was under Sidney Colvin in 1884. And in Berlin, the Kupferstichkabinett was founded in 1831; Friedrich Lippmann was the head in 1884. In reading the correspondence and the books and other publications of those curators who have described their lives, one sees that their activities consisted of acquiring collections for their institutions, purchasing entire collections; completing the works of major printmakers, that is, buying the remaining Schongauers, the remaining Dürers, the remaining Rembrandts that they missed; and ordering the rapidly growing collections that became thus deposited in institutions in order to make them more available for visitors and more useful for research. As Alfred Whitman, an assistant curator in the British Museum, described it in 1901, his life consisted in dealing with the thousands of acquisitions each year, registering them, stamping them, arranging them, and in serving public visitors, including—and his French colleagues were especially strong on this point—those incredibly tiresome official callers. It seems to have been a very popular thing, which I am happy to say is not true in Washington nowadays, that official foreign visitors, diplomatic visitors and so forth, would be routinely brought to the print cabinet in the capital city and shown beautiful drawings and prints. In fact, my colleague Walter Koschatzky tells me this is still the case in Vienna at the Albertina, so they have two boxes of special drawings set aside for these official visits! What Alfred Whitman does not mention, but we know perfectly well, is that these curators were also great scholars and devoted a large part of their lives to research on their collections and to publications.

In America, the situation was quite different. There were print collectors in America, and serious ones, since the first half of the nineteenth century. George Marsh, a Vermont congressman in Washington, sold his very large collection to the Smithsonian in 1849. That is the earliest acquisition of a major private American collection that I have found. There is at Harvard the famous Gray collection, which was donated in 1857, consisting of about five thousand prints. John Phillips's collection, which he gave to the Pennsylvania Academy in 1876, contained sixty thousand prints! There were also good dealers. As the Grolier Club's first president, Robert Hoe, said in 1880, 'There are now in our principal cities importers of and dealers in prints, in whose shops examples of the best etchings and engravings, both ancient and modern, may be had.' There was no longer a need for Americans to go to Europe to find these prints, as there had been in the first half of the century. There were certainly also large groups of prints in American museums and libraries, occasionally with adjunct or part-time staff who were deputed to oversee them. However, in 1884 there was not one single print department in America, nor one single official curator of prints. The following year, 1885, the Smithsonian founded the first American department of prints with Sylvester Rosa Koehler, an émigré from Leipzig, as its curator. In 1887, the Museum of Fine Arts in Boston established a department; in 1897, the Library of Congress and the Fogg; and finally, New York acquired its first print department in 1899 when the New York Public Library accepted the Avery collection and appointed Frank Weitenkampf its first curator.

In terms of the differences between the past and the present in America, then, clearly the major difference is the existence of curators of prints and the vast expansion of such positions, especially in the last thirty years. There has been a proliferation of print collections, not only in terms of the expansion of museums with their attendant collections of prints, but also in terms of the recognition of the utility and value of those prints that existed circumstantially in institutional collections and that now have been sorted out and used. In particular, universities and university collections have become increasingly aware of the value of fine prints as a resource for showing the entire history of art from the late Gothic period in original works of art, which they could hardly plan to do with paintings or with sculpture, or even with drawings. The rate of curatorial expansion in America can be seen from glancing at statistics on membership in the Print Council of America, the official organization for museum curators of prints who have been in the field long enough to show a serious commitment to it. The Print Council was founded in 1956 with eighteen members; ten years later it had more than twice as many; and today there are one hundred and twenty.

Beyond the existence and number of American print curators, how does the curator's approach to prints differ now from one hundred years ago? I will focus my discussion on two issues: exhibitions and acquisitions. The practice of an institution framing and hanging a public exhibition of prints began in the 1790s in Paris, just after the Revolution. It fits with a general conception of the Revolution that private treasures should be put on public view so that the democratic public could make use of them. In 1807, an assistant curator at the Bibliothèque Nationale, Jean Duchesne, gave this idea of a public exhibition a more solid foundation. He produced in frames under glass 'a selection of prints which one may consider to serve as a basic history of printmaking until the present.' He began with forty prints in his exhibition; twelve years later he had four times that number; and in 1855, there were four hundred prints on exhibition in the Bibliothèque Nationale to survey the history of printmaking.

Let me emphasize that these were not temporary exhibitions based on a specific theme. This was one permanent hanging survey of history including all schools and all periods.

In 1844, John Maberly wrote *The Print Collector*, a major book of its kind in England, in which he called for the British Museum to follow the French example. By the 1880 reissuing of Maberly's book, edited by our own Robert Hoe, Maberly's call had been answered by the British Museum with 'a constant and ever changing exhibition of the finest works' scattered through the library rooms and halls in cases with inclined glass tops. However, the first real example at the British Museum of what we call an exhibition, that is, the gathering in a contiguous space of an organized series of objects, was in a new special exhibition gallery opened in 1888. There the British Museum created the type of museum exhibition that we know today: a thematic exhibition that is also temporary. First they showed Chinese and Japanese scroll paintings, then English watercolors, then old master drawings from John Malcolm's collection, followed by the complete etchings of Rembrandt. Each of these exhibitions lasted three years. When I say the British Museum 'created' such exhibitions, I have to qualify that: the British Museum initiated them among museums. Before that there were many other examples of thematic exhibitions among commercial galleries and private institutions, not the least of which was our own Grolier Club. The Grolier Club was far ahead of any museum in having thematic exhibitions of prints. Its first exhibition, at the very first meeting of The Grolier Club on 1 May 1884, displayed 150 etchings from Dürer to Whistler and was followed in the next five years by twelve more exhibitions of prints—exhibitions that were monographic, exhibitions that were thematic, and exhibitions that were chronological, that is, the prints from a certain period.

The major difference between the present and the past, however, is not merely the existence of museum exhibitions, but the quantity. There has been an extraordinary increase in the number and the rate of exhibitions. The British Museum had one exhibition every three years in the 1890s, and Alfred Whitman complained vociferously about the amount of work that went into preparing such an exhibition. But now, in the same time span, the British Museum has ten to fifteen exhibitions. That is, not at the rate of one every three years but one every three months. There are four results of this remarkable quantitative leap. First of all, a curator's life at a major museum continues to involve acquisitions, the arrangement and preservation of the collections, and research on the collections; but it is most consistently dominated by exhibitions. First comes the selection and scheduling of exhibitions—in 1983 when the National Gallery opened our new Print and Drawing Galleries, we had twelve exhibitions of graphic art in one calendar year! Then comes the research and preparation of the individual exhibitions selected. A large part of our time is also spent with exhibition administration, including the handling of incoming loans and outgoing loans. The National Gallery, like any other major museum, lends hundreds of prints and drawings every year to dozens of exhibitions. Currently we lend to about forty exhibitions a year, both in this country and abroad. For the public, the results of this increase in exhibitions are overwhelmingly positive. Now members of the public have remarkable opportunities to view, in person and under excellent circumstances, many examples of the world's greatest art in prints and drawings brought to their home city, arranged in intelligent order, truly served on a silver platter. For museums, the higher number of exhibitions frequently involves major publicity and economic considerations, which are especially crucial to those museums that because of budgetary restrictions now have to live to some extent on their entrance fees.

The results of this increase in exhibitions for scholarship, however, strike me as the most curious and ambiguous of all. They are focused on the domination of print scholarship by exhibition catalogues. By far the most important publication outlet for scholars is now the exhibition catalogue, and the desire of scholars to publish through exhibition catalogues is one of the driving forces behind the increased number of exhibitions. The reasons are multiple. I myself believe that this is in part a reaction to a failure in timeliness on the part of periodical and book publishers. For an important scholarly article most major journals take, let us say, two years from time of submission to the time it appears. Book publishers are much worse, on the average. Therefore, the lesson is clear: an exhibition catalogue must be out, that is, in the conception of most museums, it must be out by a date certain, the opening of the exhibition; so a scholar is assured of timeliness. Remembering such professional problems as assistant professors building a bibliography to acquire tenure, then one can well understand why many scholars prefer to publish through exhibition catalogues. A second reason scholars prefer exhibition catalogues is the ease of research and writing. I think we have to be honest. Certainly, catalogues require work; there is no doubt about that. But unless the scholar takes his job extremely seriously, he will find it easier, with the small increments of bits of work, to write catalogue entries seriatim until he builds to the average one hundred items, with a nice introduction, than to think about a subject over many years and come to a coherent, complicated analysis presented in the form of a thorough book. Finally, there are what I might call the vanity and the ghost factors. The pressure within a museum to produce an exhibition catalogue on time is also a pressure to produce something on time. Once a scholar secures a role as a curator of an exhibition, let us say a guest curator, he is assured of, first of all, minimal vetting by his fellow professionals. An article or a book may be circulated to several readers. Unfavorable criticism may stop or greatly postpone its publication. Not so with an exhibition catalogue. There may be outside readers, but almost nothing they can say will stop the publication. Secondly, the scholar is assured of maximum help from all of the editorial and professional staff of the exhibiting institution. For example, much of the National Gallery's curatorial, editorial, and design staffs' time is spent cleaning up texts that are submitted to us by outside curators for exhibitions. Why not just drop such problem texts? Well, you cannot do it because of a rather ironic twist that is the result of pressure on museums for increasingly numerous loans. Because we are all besieged with requests for loans, we take the attitude that we cut down on the number of loans we send out by sending such loans only to serious exhibitions. A serious exhibition is especially one with a catalogue, a scholarly catalogue. Once a museum embarks upon an exhibition, puts it on the schedule, hires an outside curator, and, particularly, once the museum sends out the sheaf of loan letters signed by the director, there is no withdrawal. Everything must be done to take that text, whatever condition it is in, and put it into decent shape so that the museum can publish it with some pride, and certainly without embarrassment. We must produce a catalogue!

In terms of acquisitions, the difference between the past and the present strikes me not in terms of great individual items. Amazing things, of utmost world importance, have been and are still available and are being acquired by curators. Just to mention a few examples: the unique first state of Pollaiuolo's *Battle of the Naked Men*, acquired by Cleveland in 1967. As you know, Albrecht Altdorfer created the genre of pure landscape as a public art form in the West (you could hardly pick a more important genre), and he did this in a series of nine etchings about 1520. The largest and best of those etchings, of which only four impressions are known, in the best impression of the four, was acquired in 1978 by the National Gallery. Just now as we meet there is on the market a Mantegna engraving that is better than any other example of his engraving that has been for sale in this century. These works are of extraordinary importance and are equal to anything, as a single item, acquired by past curators, whether in Europe or in America.

The difference between then and now is partially in the quantity of acquired items or groups. That is, in 1884, an acquired collection at the upper end of size might range from several thousand to tens of thousands of prints. But now the larger collections that we acquire range from, say, two hundred to two thousand. The difference is mainly, though, in terms of the type of acquisition, that is, the understanding of what aspects we look for in an acquisition. A century ago, the British Museum acquired thirteen thousand prints and sketches by Cruikshank, 150,000 bookplates from Sir Wollaston Franks's collection, John Malcolm's collection of old master drawings and prints, and Frederick Crace's collection in sixty portfolios of views and plans of old London. Thus, major acquisitions included works of artistic and aesthetic value, works of further documentary value for portraying the entire *oeuvre* of an artist, works of documentary value for historical topography, and of documentary value for heraldry and personal history. Such multi-purpose building of print collections began also in the United States and continued for at least seventy-five to one hundred years. However, at the same time were sown the seeds to undo this. Those seeds were planted in the late nineteenth century with magnificent projects for publishing facsimiles of all of the prints of major early masters. We think in particular of Amand Durand's incredibly beautiful, and now very deceptive, heliogravures. From 1872 to 1878 he produced the finest, most faithful facsimiles of Rembrandt etchings, Dürer engravings, Schongauer engravings, Ostade etchings, etcetera. In the first years of the twentieth century came such projects as Loys Delteil's publication of good reproductions of every print by select modern masters. The post–World War II period saw even more extraordinary projects begun, I think, by F. W. H. Hollstein, where the intention was not just to publish the complete works of major artists, but the complete work of all artists in a certain period—all Dutch prints from 1450 to 1700, all German prints from 1400 to 1700. Now this is culminating in an absolute explosion of photographing, photocopying, and photorecording technologies. Reasonably legible reproductions have now become so easily and plentifully available that I believe there is no longer a need to create numerous print collections of an enormous volume or comprehensiveness as research resources for information on the images alone. Many people wish to consult prints for such information from images, echoing William Ivins's view of the primary role of prints at the beginning of printmaking, that is, the conveying of information. Someone who wishes to receive such information from images on issues of topography, or satire, or heraldry, or political caricature, historical portraits, and so on, may now, and soon evermore, consult published corpuses of reproductions. Or for those subjects not yet pounced upon by avid publishers of microfiches and extensive catalogues of reproductions, he may go to one of the big documentary collections, the Bibliothèque Nationale with its, whatever it is, fifteen, sixteen, eighteen million prints, or the British Museum, find the objects and get photographs or even photocopies.

My thesis, then, is that now the only dominant reason for a curator to acquire prints is not to have that image represented but to have the special qualities of that original object represented, and by far the most important of these are aesthetic qualities. I know that this is a movement still very much underway and still not clearly acknowledged by everyone, and certainly not by all curators. But I think the seeds have been planted and grown and the situation is clear. This is parallel to what happened to printmakers in the middle of the nineteenth century when photography took over the reproduction of paintings, leaving original printmaking as the primary form of the printmakers' activity. The implications are also clear for curators. There is no longer a need to embark upon numerous acquisitions of huge collections of images that are being preserved for the documentary value of their images, not even when the purpose is to have, per se, a documentary example of every print by a certain artist. Further, I believe there is an issue of curatorial responsibility. We all expend public funds. No matter whether we regard our museum as public or private or a mixture thereof, we all spend public money through our tax laws. We spend it to acquire works and we spend it to preserve works. In this context, heightened by the recent rise in prices of prints, not only do most of us not now *need* to collect prints for the information in their images; but because of their cost, I think we *should* not so collect them. It is a bad use of money. Instead of buying prints for those purposes or expending great sums to preserve numerous examples, save a few examples of each for archival reference, and for the rest use reproductions. Then we collect prints not as carriers of information alone but as art objects, with their total visual and experiential effect. This immediately leads to the question, what, beyond the information of the image, does the object have to offer? What makes it function and impress as a concrete work of art? Which leads to the question, how good is the image as an art work, its conception, composition, its draughtsmanship and expression? How good is the particular impression, its color and tone? Does it truly or in some special fashion convey the artist's ability or his intentions? How good is the physical condition—is it original or is it restored? All of which adds up to the connoisseurship of prints. The result of my thesis, then, is that the connoisseurship of prints, which many regard as an old-fashioned science whose widespread practice is long past, is for curators the most intelligent and the most responsible wave of the future.

As for the future, what will it be like to be a curator of prints a hundred years from now? What will the major differences be? I will focus my prediction in two areas. I suspect there will be major differences in acquisitions. I suspect it, but I cannot show it. In an ironic fashion, I cannot show it precisely because the field is currently just evolving towards the revival of connoisseurship that I forecast. Because of that, modern publications and the general oral knowledge of the field are totally inadequate to evaluate what is the scarcity or the availability of truly important impressions of a wide range of fine prints. Contrast that with the situation for drawings, where we can show statistically what the movement of history is. There remain now in private hands, for example, eight Leonardo drawings, whereas in 1884 there were thirty-eight. There are now only thirteen Raphaels and four Michelangelos. But we do not know, for example, how many truly fine impressions there are of Dürer's *Melancholia*, or of Baldung's chiaroscuro woodcuts. We simply do not have that information because the field is just evolving again towards that sense of the connoisseurship of the object as an art work rather than as the documentation of an image. Nevertheless, probably prints will follow the same pattern of scarcity as drawings. Thus, even though at present curators are still making major acquisitions of individual items, in the future even they will become increasingly unavailable for the most important old masters. Except, I believe, for Dürer and Rembrandt, where there continues to be, surprisingly, a very steady supply of good impressions.

The second major difference, and I think the most important difference between now and the future, will be in research. As far as one may reasonably predict now, the major factor will be a vastly changed technology for recording, organizing, transmitting, and analyzing reproductions of images. Recording may be on microfiche or the new video disk— as you know the video disk contains fifty-five thousand images on a single phonograph-record–sized object. The Bibliothèque Nationale contains between fifteen and twenty million separate prints. They currently have an intensive program to photograph them for microforms and have already finished about one million. Granted, that is only one out of fifteen or twenty. However, by comparison even with the projects of Hollstein— Hollstein was to have eight to ten thousand reproductions of Dutch prints—having a million reproductions of prints available is fantastic! The technology for transmitting these reproductions electronically and, by way of verbal descriptions of them, the ability to tie in with computers to organize and analyze these images will be phenomenal.

Unless there are major economic reasons, I assume that by 2084 all the world, certainly curators all over the world, should be able to sit at a visual terminal at home or in the office and have access to a world-wide data base of prints in all major collections. The research possibilities are exciting and numerous. As examples, I will mention four different types. The census material that will be available to us will be extraordinary. To know where certain prints are, where they can be seen in person if we need to. To be able to document the quantity of prints, to be able to talk intelligently about the rarity of certain types of prints, and to know just what one is talking about, at least in terms of surviving impressions. To know that there are just so many impressions of a certain print. Why do certain Rembrandt etchings appear so plentiful in good impressions, whereas others appear so rare? Such an issue can really be most intelligently addressed after we have this technology available. For a second type of research, think of the enhanced ability to study images in relationship to each other. To study the visual sources for a particular artist, to be able to start with, say, a Beham woodcut of a peasant wedding dance and by means of a computer hookup through verbal descriptions of all prints available in programmed collections to be able to call up onto the screen, say, all woodcuts produced in Germany between 1520 and 1550 of peasant dances. To see how that Beham fits in with that total environment of printed images will be an extraordinary facility. Third, the attribution of anonymous works, currently being explored by Professor Jacques Thullier at the Institut de France, is one of the most important results of these new technologies. Suppose in Leningrad you have a print that shows an old man with a white beard seated by a fireplace, but it is torn, there is no signature, you have no idea what it is. By means of your verbal analysis, you call up an expandable range of similar images, and, sure enough, you come to the same one and find it is Thomas Nast's wood engraving of Santa Claus. But for a curator working in Leningrad, Thomas Nast's image of Santa Claus might be a thing as removed as certain details of African art would be for American curators. Finally, even research into artists' changes and variations in print impressions will be so much easier. I remember in the late sixties when I was engaged in very hefty research, carrying around increasingly large numbers of detailed photographs to study the complex revisions in the lines of Piranesi's *Carceri* etchings. At the Met talking with Hyatt Mayor, we were comparing notes on how primitive this technology was. We presumed that in the future, certainly a

ANDREW ROBISON

hundred years from now, one could make use of the advances of our defense department in analyzing high-altitude or satellite photographs by superimposing one transparent photograph over another in order to highlight the changes so that we can see where a foreign power has built another road to a hole in the ground and suspect that perhaps there is a missile emplacement there. Think of what such technology would mean for studying Rembrandt's states. You get equivalently good photographs of, let us say, a thousand impressions—why not?—and have them super-imposed electronically so that the changes are highlighted. What an ex-traordinary facility will be available to the researcher of the future, even for what for me is the most interesting aspect of different impressions, the subtle variations of early impressions. For example, we could put real force into the question what was the intention of Dürer in printing the *Melancholia*? Why do we see so many silvery impressions? Is that really what he wanted? Let us locate and correlate lots of impressions, vast num-bers, and then document the variations so that we can talk intelligently about the most interesting variations in the finest works of art. Thus the extraordinary technology of the future should even help to facilitate the revival and the serious enhancement of solid connoisseurship!

A Print Collector's View

WALTER BAREISS

Before addressing myself to the theme 'Then, Now, and Tomorrow' from the point of view of a print, drawing, and illustrated-book collector, I should tell you something about my own development as a collector since what I have to say later will to a great extent be colored by my own experience.

My collecting life covers just about half the one hundred years of The Grolier Club. In the spring of 1933, with the help of my father, I made my first purchase: a Picasso print titled *The Dance of Salome*. I had seen it in the window of an art dealer in Zurich and passed it almost daily on my way home from school. So began my fifty years as a patient suffering from the pleasant disease of art collecting. It is an enjoyable addiction and one that, like other addictions, tends to keep one cash broke. And just as one rarely plans to become addicted to anything, so one rarely *plans* to become a collector; after a time, one simply turns out to *be* one.

I believe I am an old-fashioned collector, one who goes far afield and avoids, if at all possible, specializing too much. This brings us to the first part of our theme, 'then and now.' If in the following remarks I make some subjective value judgments, please forgive me.

Let us look first at the 'then': we can consider the period from 1884 to 1950 as one since during that time changes in the collecting world were more often the results of wars, recessions, political turmoil, and possibly even population shifts, than of fundamental differences in interest or philosophy.

We all know that there is not a day when one cannot find for little money something extraordinary in the field of graphics or books—provided one has knowledge, experience, sensitivity, and, of course, a good memory. It remains true, and always will, that the best way to learn to collect is to look and look and look some more. This was just as true before the World Wars as it is today, but time moved more slowly then, and with it, changes in education, exposure, and taste. Prices did not go up—and sometimes down—as rapidly then as during the past thirty years. Of course, there were exceptions, such as that of Mrs. Havemayer and the Ventes Degas, which drove Degas prices up dramatically.

The rich elite and their dealers had a corner on the market. And the collecting of paintings, sculptures, decorative arts, and, to a lesser extent, old master drawings and prints was not so much an investment, albeit a pleasant one, as a way of satisfying the desire for prestige and of competing with one's peers. As magnificent a small, highly selective, and varied collection as that of Russell Allen in Boston, or the all-encompassing one of Lessing Rosenwald, could probably not be assembled again today.

To understand the change, we must look at the 'now': collectors today are a different breed from those at the turn of the century and throughout the two World Wars. First of all, there are more of them. More travel, voluntary and involuntary, and greater education in general and greater availability of excellent training in art history specifically have clearly stimulated an interest in art collecting for a completely new group of people.

In addition, the growing size of the student body all over the free world and the increased size of the middle class, and its ability to spend money on other than basic needs, are also responsible for the surging interest in collecting. Since 1950, people have had more money, and collecting has become less elitist. Particularly among well-rounded, younger people, a desire to substitute spiritual values for material goods has manifested itself in an interest in art and art history. With it has come art purchasing, and from pure accumulation and possession, in many cases, it has drifted into art collecting.

Indeed, there is the same sense of revolution in art collecting as in life in general. As people began to challenge old values, there were signs among collectors—as far back as the 1920s—of an aggressive stance against the art of the past. This general trend toward trying to build something unorthodox—the emerging interest in dadaism, for example—was full blown by 1950. A close friend of mine, a well-known collector who has assembled an outstanding, highly specialized collection of classic modern art, recently argued that he would start collecting orange wrappers, since in his opinion the original art on many of them was among the best and most individualistic expressions in the field.

This revolution against the past and the consequent search for undiscovered fields has paralleled what to me is the most striking characteristic of art collecting today: specialization. Almost every collector I have met or read about recently seems to be specializing in ever-narrowing areas. Because of my own predilection, however, I am delighted to note that among museum curators the all-around collecting tradition is still alive and kicking. Even in those institutions that can because of their size or endowment afford separate curatorships for prints and illustrated books, both old and new, curators remain vitally interested, if often only vicariously, in areas outside of their own.

What is behind the trend toward specialization? For one thing, old master drawings and prints are vanishing from the marketplace because of acquisition by museums and other institutions. Add to this some permanent losses due to wars or revolutionary takeovers and you have a situation in which collectors have to go further and further afield to satisfy their addiction. They have to find areas or schools not yet touched or look at less-known artists passed over by other buyers and museums.

Art dealers, and, to a certain extent, artists, are adjusting to, if not catering to, this specialization. Because of vanishing supplies of old masters, as well as higher prices and limited finances, dealers are constantly searching for something new. In some instances, they are becoming even more specialized than their customers. Artists have noted that the ever-increasing pool of collectors, albeit with lesser financial resources, looks more and more to large prints to take the place of paintings. Today's artists also realize that they must think of new ways of doing things, new conceptions, to compete for dealers and collectors. Consequently, color and other surface effects are 'in,' while black and white has become an 'also ran.'

Because of the multitude of contemporary artists, a collector just beginning to put his toe into the fascinating, exciting, and murky waters of collecting cannot help but concentrate on a narrow area and thus become more and more specialized. Most collectors today are not members of the leisure class; they have jobs and do not have the time to do research in a wide variety of areas. The wealthier collectors may still assemble drawings or prints worth millions by old masters and 'name' modern artists, while the poorer or more adventurous may find edition prints, illustrated books, or drawings by not-yet-established contemporary artists more to their liking.

But even the rich perforce have to specialize, for obvious reasons. The Picasso *Dance of Salome*, which I mentioned earlier, was bought in the gallery Actuarius in Zurich in 1933 for fifty Swiss francs, or about twelve dollars. Even if we accept that today's dollar is worth only one-fiftieth of the 1933 dollar, or two cents, then that print today should sell for about six hundred dollars. But we all know that's not so—a good copy of the *Dance of Salome* would bring ten times that, about six thousand dollars. As a result, collectors today need more than money. They also need confidence, knowledge, and perseverance. Isn't it wonderful that confidence and knowledge come first and second, and money last?

The spectacular price increases, the constant publicity, and the speed of change have become disruptive influences on the life of the collector. The result: art has become for many more of an investment than an aesthetic pleasure. While few collectors consider themselves 'art investors,' it is hard for anyone to avoid taking a sideways peek at the auction results or Souren Melekian's column in the *International Herald Tribune* and asking himself, 'How am I doing?' In short, works of art begin to look like so many dollar bills, rather than the beautiful objects they are.

Beautiful objects! This is clearly an old-fashioned idea. Beauty is often conceived nowadays as something to be fought, not only by the collector, but by the artist. Although not actually spelled out, this attitude is often apparent.

I once had the opportunity to talk with Hans Arp shortly after I purchased a beautiful collage from his dada period. Having come to the dealer's to fix the frame, he insisted the collage had nothing to do with beauty but was completely unplanned and happenstance—a 'casual toss of paper scraps.' I didn't argue, but I have thought ever since that, despite their protestations, men like Arp, Schwitters, and, now, Beuys simply did not want to accept the fact that they were wonderful artists in the aesthetic sense.

The same is true today of many collectors who believe beauty is decadent. They, too, will find when they look back that, if they collected well, they have built a thing of beauty—even if that's not what they set out to do in forming the collection.

In addition to skyrocketing prices, the lack of space, and the explosion in the quantity of modern art, there are other factors underlying the trend toward specialization. Growing populism and socialist philosophy, becoming stronger in the Western, or so-called free, world since the 1950s, no doubt have a great deal to do with changing collecting habits. I doubt that guilt feelings plagued the great collectors of the past. I can't imagine that the Medicis or J. P. Morgan, Jr., worried about the feelings of their less fortunate contemporaries when they amassed magnificent collections and housed them in equally magnificent buildings.

Today's collectors, after satisfying their cravings to collect and achieving the prestige they desire, often announce that they are leaving their art to a museum or actually give it away during their lifetimes. Some even state they are collecting for the public. This trend seems particularly prevalent in the United States but less so in Europe and, possibly, in the Far East, where there are lower inheritance taxes, resulting in less of an incentive to make gifts to institutions.

The American attitude again contributes to making today's collections more specialized, less personal, and, perhaps, more perfectionistic—for example, the perfect Munch collection. Those collectors who feel differently remain anonymous, collecting in private and often in a relatively limited space. For them, the drawing and print fields are perfect vehicles for assuaging their collecting instincts and satisfying their cravings for beauty.

The technical possibilities of modern printmaking are such that even the most extreme desire for sensationalism and adventure can be satisfied. Collectors can choose lithographs, etchings, engravings, wood- or lino-cuts, or silk-screen prints—or those made by mixing techniques. They can find anything from miniature prints in black and white to three-dimensional colored objects forty square feet and larger.

To summarize the 'now and then': from all-around graphic collections often attached to large diversified art collections such as the Morgan or Lehman, we have arrived at smaller, specialized collections, assembled by infinitely larger numbers of people, who often are better educated and more knowledgeable in their field than the collectors of the past. Some collections amassed in Europe during the past fifty to sixty years could probably never have been assembled in the United States, and comparable ones will probably never be assembled anywhere in the world.

As an example, I have in mind the collection of Frits Lugt, whom I had the pleasure of knowing during and shortly after the Second World War. His collection is now at the Institute Hollandaise in Paris. Lugt was probably the essence of the connoisseur-collector and art historian. His book *Les Marques de Collections de Dessins et d'Estampes* is still an essential standard work for all collectors of old master drawings and prints. The quality and scope of his collection is so great that even now only few can really judge its importance. Not only his Dutch drawings and prints, but also the Italian ones and others, are hard to be believed.

Even today, in Europe, some diversified collections are possible. Just recently I saw a small but beautiful collection comprised of old master prints and drawings, some outstanding twentieth-century paintings, and African art—all being collected at the same time.

Where does this leave us? Probably with a continuation of the current trend: more and more first-class drawings and prints continue to find their way into institutions and, so, become unavailable to collectors. Space continues to become scarcer and private curating services to become increasingly expensive. Despite all this, the wish for prestige and capital gains as well as the craving for beauty and rarity continue unabated.

Despite all this, I feel a certain optimism that in the long run a certain reaction will occur. I foresee the following developments: price increases will become less extreme, at most keeping pace with inflation, as the old masters disappear from the market and the quantity of offerings of contemporary artists, especially prints and drawings, increases dramatically. People will then collect less for investment purposes and more for individual philosophic and aesthetic reasons and, in the end, for personal enjoyment.

A collector may become an art appreciator first and an accumulator second. As the possibility of acquiring a complete or almost complete series of Picasso, Munch, or Matisse prints vanishes, the collector will be able to enjoy a sketchy drawing hanging or lying in a portfolio beside a print by the same artist.

To go even further, a collection might consist of pieces of decorative art of the past and present together with a few pieces of good furniture. There might be a few paintings, old or new, on the walls and a few contemporary or ethnological sculptures. A small number of carefully selected drawings, prints, and illustrated books might round out the collection—one amassed less for prestige, investment, or the need for completeness than for personal pleasure, stimulation, and even a sense of history.

A Print Dealer's View

EBERHARD W. KORNFELD

The founding year of The Grolier Club was 1884. A booming year in the United States and, also, in Europe. 1865 had seen the end of the war in the United States, and in 1871 Europe followed suit. Industrial development was in full flow; it was the time of nonstop invention, the time of the making of big fortunes that even today are still in evidence. Wealth and times of industrial boom tend to increase interest in culture. It is no coincidence that The Grolier Club was founded at this time. On one side, the founding members were certainly idealists, but on the other hand, they were also 'proud possessors' trying to create a stage from which their collections, of which they had reason to be proud, could be shown both to fellow enthusiasts and to a larger section of the public.

Although I am supposed to give you a summary of the story of collecting of and dealing in prints and drawings during the last one hundred years, I would like to go further back to remind you that already in the sixteenth century there were important dealers who distinguished themselves in the fields of drawings and fine prints. Unfortunately, we know none of the names of these dealers. Often the artist himself acted as his own dealer; Dürer sold his own engravings at fairs and during his travels. However, a collection like the one of the German Emperor Maximilian I would have been impossible without the active help of his chancellor, Treitzsauerwein, who acted as a kind of art dealer. If Bonifacius and Basilius Amerbach of Basel—father and son active as collectors from about 1520 to 1570, whose collection was bought by the city of Basel in 1661— had not had agents spread all over Europe, then this collection could not have been of the same importance.

Clement de Jonghe of Amsterdam was probably one of the most important graphic-art dealers in the Netherlands in the seventeenth century. He had his gallery on the Kalverstraat and was active in the world of art dealing from about 1640 until his death in 1679. After his death, an inventory was made from which we have our first detailed knowledge of Rembrandt's graphics.

In 1651 Rembrandt had portrayed this important personage in an etching overworked with drypoint, and Clement de Jonghe had always done his utmost for Rembrandt's drawings and prints. It was Clement de Jonghe who supplied Rembrandt with Italian engravings of the sixteenth and seventeenth centuries in order to satisfy the artist's passion for collecting. As a result of this passion, Rembrandt was forced to declare bankruptcy in 1656. The resulting auction sale of his collection, held in an inn on Kalverstraat in Amsterdam, took place in December 1657 and was an important event. There were posters all over the city touting the sale for prospective purchasers (now only one of these posters exists, in the print room of the British Museum in London). The poster read 'Sagets vort,' which loosely translates as 'Spread the word.' The auctioneer, Thomas Haaring, was also very famous. In spite of the difficult circumstances, Rembrandt and Haaring were friends, and Rembrandt made an etching of him, which is unfortunately very rare.

The next important event in the field of art auctions took place over one hundred years later when the Paris art dealer Pierre François Basan auctioned the famous Mariette collection in 1775. This was the breaking up of a collection that had been accumulated by generations of dealers devoted to this influential family. The sale certainly also included the last stock of the Mariette gallery and was the end of a long tradition. Pierre Mariette, born around 1600, was the father of the dynasty. With two wives, both daughters of influential bookdealers, he had sixteen children, but only one is important for us, his son Pierre Mariette II, born in 1633. He carried on family traditions, both by continuing to run the business and by marrying a daughter of a bookdealer. His wife was the widow of the dealer François Langlois who had been portrayed by van Dyck and had also worked as an agent of the earl of Arundel. Their son Jean Mariette, born in 1660, also continued the family tradition; he was the father of Pierre Jean Mariette, born in 1694, who brought the importance of the great family of dealers to its zenith. He was one of the most important dealers, collectors, and art historians of his time. The whole world of collecting in France in the eighteenth century was dominated by this man. He influenced many people, among them Jean Crozat, who met Pierre Jean Mariette in 1720. The great dealer died in 1774 at the age of eighty, and in the next year his collection came up for auction under the direction of P. F. Basan, who himself was the father of the next important dynasty of Parisian art dealers.

The catalogue of the auction of the Mariette collection does not only have an incredibly abundant content—a total of 1,488 lots, some of them consisting of several pieces—but is itself a work of art and precious to the bibliophile. The title-page is by Moreau le Jeune and the frontispiece—a tribute to the collector—is etched by Choffard after a drawing by Cochin. The section of Rembrandt prints contains over 420 etchings, the majority of excellent quality. The auction exhibition lasted for only eight days; the auction itself ran from 15 November 1775 until 30 January 1776, with short interruptions for the holidays. The turnover was enormous, amounting to the sum of 288,500 livres. One of the most important buyers was Louis XVI, who acquired 1,061 drawings for his collection in the Louvre, his bill totaling 58,000 livres. What an 'embarras de richesse'!

When the French Revolution broke out in 1789, the big collections suffered changes. Several noble families lost significant parts of their collections, which then found themselves forming the bases of new collections belonging to the bourgeoisie and to some of the members of the new Napoleonic aristocracy. But in spite of the big changes in France, the auction activity in Paris continued. When the collection of Jean-Guillaume Alibert was sold in 1803, the auction catalogue gives the dates of the duration of the auction from '5th to 15th Floréal in the XI year of the Revolution,' but also translates the corresponding dates as 'April 25th to May 5th, 1803.'

In the nineteenth century, there was an increasing awareness that the collecting possibilities of drawings and graphics were becoming more and more limited. When The Grolier Club was founded in 1884, the house that I run today was already twenty years old. Heinrich Georg Gutekunst, the son of a painter, had decided in 1864 to set up his own gallery in Stuttgart. He had been trained by Goupil & Cie in Paris and was so talented that by the age of twenty-four he was sent to London to run their English branch. He remained there until 1 October 1864, when he opened his own gallery in Stuttgart and published the first catalogue of his stock. He was the first dealer to recognize the difficulties of finding good quality stock and, therefore, wrote in the foreword of the catalogue:

> Despite the ever-increasing difficulty of finding beautiful examples
> of masterpieces of the old German, Dutch, and Italian schools, I
> flatter myself with the hope that this catalogue offers desirable
> works to the respected art enthusiast, and that the marvelous pieces
> of our new era will find numerous admirers who will display them
> at their homes.

When I look through the catalogues of today, and compare them with the catalogues that Gutekunst published until his retirement in 1914, and think about his warning, then I wonder what the catalogues will contain in one hundred years.

The quality and quantity of Gutekunst's catalogues are quite incredible. Thanks to a well-informed circle of collectors, minimal description of the properties was required. Early states of the most beautiful prints by Dürer and Rembrandt and rich choices of prints of the fifteenth century were all present next to drawings by Burkmair, Dürer, Hirschvogel, Rembrandt, Raphael, van Dyck, and Rubens—all of superb quality. Collections that stir up great memories—those of Keller, Durazzo, Hebich, Weigel, Angiolini, Straeter, Habich, Cornill d'Orville, Waldburg-Wolfegg, Novak, Artaria, Griesebach, Rumpf, Lanna, and Theobald (to mention just the most important)—all passed through the hand of this aristocrat of his trade.

In 1895, the sale of the Milanese Luigi Angiolini's collection was dispersed through a catalogue of nearly 4,000 lots containing 13 Masters ES;

64 Israel van Meckenems; 13 Jean Duvets; 190 Rembrandts; and 165 Dürers, the sets of engravings and woodcuts all in complete early editions and forming one lot each.

This was followed in 1898 by the sale of the Dr. August Straeter collection: among a very large selection of Dutch drawings from the seventeenth century there were seven drawings by Rembrandt, and in the print section 130 Dürers, again all complete sets and each forming only one lot; 250 prints by Rembrandt, including the portrait of Clement de Jonghe in four different states. Massaloff, the Russian collector, payed 5,300 marks for the portrait of the old Haaring, today equivalent to over 70,000 dollars.

1909 saw the auction sale of the first part of the collection of Baron Adalbert von Lanna from Prague. This collection was especially rich in German masters of the first part of the sixteenth century, containing nearly complete works by Aldegrever, Altdorfer, Hans Baldung Grien, Barthel and Hans Sebald Beham, the two Cranachs, and even Schongauer. For Dürer nearly none of the Bartsch numbers were missing, the same as for Lucas van Leyden or Rembrandt. A small selection of the Rembrandts offered was *The Presentation in the Temple*, Bartsch 50, for 7,100 marks; *The Ecce Homo*, Bartsch 76, fifth state, 8,300 marks; *Clement de Jonghe*, Bartsch 272, first state, 7,400 marks; *The Young Haaring*, Bartsch 275, second state, 6,350 marks; and *The Big Coppenol*, Bartsch 283, third state, which reached the incredible price of 14,100 marks. However, even in this large Rembrandt collection the portrait of the inspector Arnold Tholinx, Bartsch 284, was missing.

In 1910, the second part of the Lanna collection, consisting mainly of the drawings, was auctioned. A few names: Altdorfer, Dirk Bouts, the drawing *Justice* by Pieter Brueghel, two great works by Canaletto, and an important drawing by Ghirlandajo. Included in this sale were seventeen drawings by Dürer, one of which was the most important piece of the entire collection: the black-ink drawing for the engraving *Adam and Eve* in pen and brush. The Ghirlandajo and the Dürer were both bought by Pierpont Morgan.

Morgan paid 67,200 marks for the Dürer drawing. If one calculates that an average employee in Germany in 1910 was paid about 150 marks—equivalent today in the United States to 2,000 dollars—then the price paid for this Dürer is equivalent to 900,000 dollars in today's terms. Another high price for a drawing by Dürer was paid by Colnaghi's in London for *The Kneeling Man*, a sketch of a figure for an important painting. The price reached was 31,200 marks, over 420,000 dollars today.

Other examples from that sale are the great Watteau drawing for 4,200 marks; a study of a head by Schongauer for 3,850 marks; twelve drawings by Rembrandt, ten still accepted as genuine today; the Pisanello drawing for 12,500 marks; the great drawing by Mantegna, bought by Danlos from Paris for 20,000 marks; but the wonderful drawing by Guardi of the Campo S. Giovanni e Paolo in Venice in comparison fetched only 2,100 marks.

We still keep in our archives the auctioneer's copies of the catalogues of all those sales; here are a few examples of names of buyers still all relatively famous today: Artaria, Danlos, Meder from Berlin, Boerner, Obach, Colnaghi's, Stroelin, Rodrigues, Gus Mayer, Rosenthal, Massaloff, Friedländer, Lehrs, van Bastelaer, Hofsteede de Groot, Curtis, Stechow, Keppel, Pierpont Morgan, and Delâcre.

After the sale of the second part of the Lanna collection, Heinrich Georg Gutekunst retired and handed over his business in Stuttgart to his partner, Wilhelm A. Gaiser, who kept in close contact with Gutekunst's two sons who were working in London: Otto Gutekunst, who, together with Gus Mayer, had taken over the famous Colnaghi's, and Richard Gutekunst, who had his own business in Grafton Street.

From 1910 to 1914, the last cards were played in Stuttgart with the sales of the collections of Theobald, Gellatly, Baldinger, Rumpf, Peltzer, and Stroganoff. Then, in 1914, the great breakdown came. Wilhelm A. Gaiser died in that year, and the famous house H. G. Gutekunst came to an end. A new tradition started in Bern in 1919, when H. G. Gutekunst's son Richard, in collaboration with August Klipstein, opened the gallery Gutekunst and Klipstein. However, the old tradition of auction sales was not taken up again until 1934, when Richard Gutekunst had retired from the business.

Before we look at the great sales after 1920, let us have a glance at the great collectors and important auction sales in Russia, Holland, France, and, particularly, England, where Sotheby's and Christie's, founded in 1744 and 1766, kept an active role in presenting prints and drawings to collectors and dealers during the whole of the nineteenth century.

In Russia, the Empress Catharina II was a very notable collector in the second part of the eighteenth century. A contemporary Dutch collector, Ploos van Amstel, was of great significance not only as a collector but also as the creator of the new technique to produce excellent reproductions of drawings. In France, after the Revolution and the Napoleonic times, came the great era of the bourgeois collections. Here fit in the names like the Concourt brothers, Philipp Burty, Albert Goupil, A. Beurdeley, A. Firmin-Didot, and Baron Edmond de Rothschild.

The eighteenth and nineteenth centuries saw the high point of the collections of the English landed gentry. No important family missed out on building up a collection; paintings were the most popular items, but prints and drawings were not ignored. The turn of the nineteenth century brought with it changes: collections were no longer being expanded; on the contrary, it was with some difficulty that some collections managed to be held together. The matter deteriorated further after 1945 because of unfavorable tax laws. The English dealers and auction houses lived for decades from this seemingly never-ending flood.

I would like to bring to your notice two important print auctions around 1900—the sales of the R. S. Holford collection in 1893 at Christie's in London and the Alfred Hubert collection in 1909 at the Hotel Drouot in Paris. Both collections were of legendary quality. At these auctions, surprisingly high prices were fetched for prints that since then have only very infrequently been seen on the market.

Highlights from the Rembrandt section of the Holford sale were the following:

· *Rembrandt Leaning on a Sabre* (today, *Self Portrait with Plumed Cap and Lowered Sabre*), Bartsch 23, first state, with the following text in the catalogue: 'Only four exist in the first state, and as three of these are in National collections, this is the only one that can ever be sold.' The price: 2,000 pounds.

· *Christ Healing the Sick*, called the 'Hundred Guilder Print,' Bartsch

74, first state, from the collections Hibbert and Esdaile, on Japan paper, the last of the nine copies of this state to be sold, bought by Edmond de Rothschild for 1,750 pounds.

· *The Portrait of Ephraim Bonus*, Bartsch 278, also the first state, one of three copies known, the other two already in public collections in London and Paris, for a surprisingly high price of 1,950 pounds, also bought by Baron Edmond de Rothschild.

· *The Portrait of the Inspector Arnold Tholinx*, Bartsch 284, in the second state, fetched only 530 pounds. The Amsterdam print room possesses no copy even today.

The very important sale of the Albert Hubert collection, under the direction of the Parisian expert and dealer Danlos, brought sensational prices for a few Rembrandts:

· *The Landscape with Trees, Farm Buildings and a Tower*, Bartsch 223, in the first state, 51,700 francs.

· *The Portrait of the Bourgermaster Jan Six*, Bartsch 285, second state, from the collections Aylesford, Hawkins, and Holford, for 78,100 francs. This is equivalent today to over 1,040,000 dollars!

· And, again, an outstanding copy of the so-called 'Hundred Guilder Print,' Bartsch 74, on Japan paper, but only in the second state, 67,650 francs, today over 900,000 dollars!

And now coming to the time after the First World War, we must look at the great period of the Leipzig firm of C. G. Boerner, which had existed since 1826 but had not started its big activity as an auction house for prints and drawings until 1920, beginning with the famous sale of the Paul Davidsohn collection, presented in 1920 and 1921 in three important auction sales and described in three voluminous catalogues. The prices of these sales are misleading, as the German mark had already started its devaluation, which continued until November 1923, when one million marks would buy one kilo of bread. Therefore, all prices in German auction sales until the end of 1923 are irrelevant. Real art dealing started again only in 1924. Hans Boerner, who had been a partner of the Viennese art dealer Gustav Nebehay, took advantage of the disappearance of the old house of H. G. Gutekunst and started to dominate the auction scene of old master print collections. From 1924, many collections passed through the house of C. G. Boerner and many important names can be found in its catalogues. However, from 1933 onwards, activity was dampened due to political circumstances. In 1945, the firm restarted, first in Leipzig and then in Düsseldorf; this time, however, restricted to making stock catalogues, with no further auction activities.

The Boerner auctions in the years after 1924 started with the important groups of duplicates from the Albertina. In the aftermath of the war, the Albertina collection was combined with the print collection of the Imperial Library of the Habsburgs and one single collection formed. As a result of this combination, a large number of duplicates came on the market and were sold in different Boerner sales, followed by the sales of the Wünsch woodcut collection, the collections of Duke Wenzel von Nostiz-Rieneck, Alfred Morrison, and von Hagen, important parts of the Royal collection of Frederick August II of Saxony, and the collections of Passavant-Gontard and Model. And in 1930 and 1931, as a great surprise, came important parts of the prints and drawings collection from the Eremitage in Leningrad, sold by the Russian government. In the same years, the great collections of drawings formed by Geheimrat Ehlers from Göttingen, Dr. Gaa in Mannheim, and, most importantly, Dr. Cornelius Hofstede de Groot from The Hague came up for auction. From 1932 to 1937 were sold the collections of York von Wartenburg, Fürstenberg from Donaueschingen, Waldburg-Wolfegg, and the duke of Oettingen-Wallerstein. Many important collections were built up during this period; I mention the great collection of Lessing Rosenwald, who sent the Philadelphia dealer Bressler to many of the Leipzig sales; the Rembrandt collection of Isaac de Brujn; and, to be mentioned before all, the outstanding collection of Frits Lugt. (Significantly, all three are today in public collections.)

The quality and quantity of these auctions were such that they influenced the market and collectors' activity for a whole generation. Most believed that it would continue like this forever and failed to consider that they were living on art accumulated throughout centuries—a supply that would gradually dry up. The prices before 1914 were very much higher than those after 1929, when prices were greatly influenced by the world depression. During this period there were so many works of art on the market that they could not all be absorbed by the museums and dealers. Collectors in those days could buy at a good price, but no dealer made his fortune, not even the Boerners, who held a key position in the market.

I come now to the years after 1945, an era in which I have lived and to which I have contributed. The years until 1960 were similar to the early 1930s; the war had caused the breaking up of many old collections. In the United States, the collections of McVitty, Johnson, and Whittemore (among others) came on the market. In Europe, it was mainly the large collections of drawings and prints of the duke of Liechtenstein; the collections of Robinow, Harrach, Curtis, Thomas, and Weisbach; and the remaining parts of the York von Wartenburg family collection. Then, around 1960, came an end of an epoch, and big old collections have since only rarely been seen on the market. The resulting scarcity of pieces pushed prices up, and, also, museums in the United States suddenly started buying up more prints and drawings, which left the market with even fewer. This development continues and will certainly leave its mark on the situation in the coming years. The competition for drawings and prints will become increasingly fiercer.

For art dealers, it is now practically impossible to specialize. I hardly dare to train young people in my house exclusively in the field of old masters, as it is evident that in a few years it will be impossible to run a specialized business in this field, for the commercial opportunities will be too small. I remember my first visit to Gus Mayer at Colnaghi's in London in 1947. He showed me boxes of Rembrandt prints with an apology: 'I'm sorry; quite a few Bartsch numbers are missing.' However, he actually had about two hundred prints in his boxes. Today, we are glad if we can offer ten or fifteen Rembrandts. A similar problem exists for old master drawings.

So today we have the situation that the old-fashioned dealer in old master prints has to face the fact of having to include the so-called 'classical modern period' in his stock, starting with Goya and including the great range of the French and German prints of the nineteenth and twentieth centuries, up to and including Matisse and Picasso.

I myself follow this reasoning in the field of drawings and prints and find that modern art is a natural progression following from old masters.

On the other hand, I feel that all art, developing over the centuries under different influences, is essentially unified and results from a constant human aim.

As an art dealer, I feel the obligation to research fully the works that are entrusted to me and not just deal with them. I find it important to be acquainted with the history of art and art dealing. The knowledge of former generations of art dealers provides useful sources of information. Continuing association with art is a fascinating field, and I am very happy that I have been able to publish books on artists whom I particularly admire, such as Klee, Chagall, Signac, Picasso, and Kirchner. At present, we are concluding in my house the new catalogue raisonné of the graphic works of Gauguin, which is the work of three authors: Elizabeth Mongan, the unforgettable Harold Joachim, and myself.

Since the nineteenth century, the international circle of dealers in old graphics (mostly including the nineteenth and twentieth centuries) has diminished. Although we are serious competitors, we are all on friendly terms. There are now scarcely more than twenty of us. I would like to mention, from the United States, Bob Light, David Tunick, Ray Lewis, and Lucien Goldschmidt; in France, Hubert Prouté and Pierre Michel; in England, Adrian Eeles, the Colnaghi's, and the Barnards; in Germany, C. G. Boerner, Rolf Kistner, and Helmuth Rumbler; and in Switzerland, my colleague August Laube.

What each and every one of us would like is to find and to offer a great collection!

An Artist's View of Prints

FRANK STELLA

I cannot be presumptuous talking to you about prints today because I really do not know anything about them. I felt I knew something about art history before I started making paintings and that part of my learning about how to paint was knowing the history of painting—they were in some senses the same thing. I never expected to make prints. It was not part of my ambition, or even of my understanding. Even prints by other painters I admire have been somewhat foreign to me. I like Mondrian a lot and his sort of modernism and abstraction are things that are very important to me, but I cannot remember having seen a print by Mondrian. I have seen a few woodcuts and lithographs by Kandinsky, but I cannot imagine Kandinsky as an involved printmaker. To get back to Mondrian, there is a certain irony in this because Mondrian's images have been reproduced more widely than any other images I can think of. The images may be very difficult to print as fine art, but on the other hand it has been very easy to deal with them commercially and socially. They have become part of the fabric of society, seen nearly everywhere on dresses and upholstery.

Painting and printing do not necessarily go together, and the art of fine printing is often very divorced from the practice of fine art, especially in contemporary terms. In my own experience, I was probably halfway through a painting career before I was asked to make prints. I honestly didn't have much interest in them. But as things have gone, printing, for me, has picked up tremendous momentum in terms of fine art reproduction or fine art printing, whatever you want to call it (I notice there has been a distinction made between printing and printmaking, but I use the word 'printing' to describe what I do because I take what I do to be printing in the sense that it is involved with the process as much as it is with the result). My experience with printing has been for the most part what is called 'fine arts' printing, but I am perfectly willing to use whatever commercial techniques are available. So although I hope to make art in the end, I will use anything to make it. For me, printing is essentially about ink and paper; you have to take ink, and you have to put it on a surface, and the most conventional thing to put it on is paper. We have the technique, and we also have the imagination, to allow artists to print on anything; nothing stops an artist from printing on mylar, exotic foils, or metal, but still the gut issue in printing seems to be ink and paper. Our sense of what a good print is and what is good about printing is really bound to our notion of what is good on paper. I think it would be very hard to establish a set of aesthetic standards that would apply to mylar or metal foil. But we all have an idea about what ink is supposed to be on paper, and what line is supposed to do, and how the surface of the paper is supposed to be orchestrated.

An important issue that the artist must decide is how the ink will be located on the paper. Will it be on top of the surface, halfway in, or all the way through to the other side? How far are you going to penetrate the surface? Arrangement of the image on the sheet and the method of ink application are two variables the artist can use to overcome some of the limitations on printing. Another issue is the color of the inks, but I do not think this is a basic issue. Black and white is still the story of printing. Only very recently has printing in the West had much sense of, or use for, color because previously color was treated from a distance, and I think the artist felt it was unnecessary and really didn't want it. In my humble opinion, I don't think the West has been very good in color printing until recently. Color was actually a later application in printing as far as the Western artist was concerned; he conceived a print as a black and white graphic image, and then a lot of people encouraged him to put more color in it. My father, in fact, when he first came to see the black paintings, said, 'Well, I don't know; I don't like them all that much, and for sure they need more color.' I think this happens a lot in printing, at least with many prints that I've done.

I have found that the limits of printing really define its problems. Two obvious limitations are paper size and machinery. You can get around the size of the printing bed somewhat, but it is very hard to get around the size of the paper. You don't necessarily want your gesture limited by the size of a piece of paper. One can print half the sheet, turn it around and print the other half and gain some control over the length, but the width remains limited. This is a reflection of what printing has been about for so long, a sheet of paper. There are ways to get around the limits of the sheet of paper and defeat the sense of boundaries by shaping or penetrating it. Relief and collage offer opportunities for making the size of the paper moot. I find relief printing is particularly powerful.

Even the essence of printing is limiting in a way. An impression is literally what printing is all about; the artist is literally pressing ink into paper in order to create an image that someone will want to look at. The image is everything, it is the feel, the sense of the whole, but one of the most difficult things in printing is to orchestrate the whole and make a single forceful impression that conveys a sense of printing. I think that is what most good artists work at, and yet it is not enough to produce a forceful black and white image applied properly to paper. That is *just* printing, and it should be more; it should be art. It is as though it should be more like a painting. However, agreement on what the aim of printing is supposed to be remains a problem. For the audience, printing is mostly reproductive information, and the problem for the artist is how to meet this demand and also achieve a work of art. After all, the artist does not want to give in totally to the fact that he is only supplying information and only reproducing an image. He wants some sense of viability. An artist doesn't go to the trouble of making an image and reproducing it a hundred times to have it be a hundred dead pieces of paper. This is one reason that artists feel there is a tremendous pressure in printing that is not on individual work. For example, with a painting, you can take your chances; if it is lousy, it is lousy—it is not going to be done over and over again to haunt you. Some people may find it easy, but I find it a little difficult to make an image sustain the weight of reproduction, to make something I want to see a hundred times.

An underlying issue that people worry about is the question of who actually does the work of producing the print. The retort to this, of course, is 'Do we care?' There is the machine, there is the artist, there is the artisan, there is the publisher—and a lot of other people involved as well. We want to know if the finished print can overcome the varied circumstances of its creation by many hands. Is the print going to work for all the people involved and for everyone else? Here is where the mystique of technique comes in; we want to know where the artist is in the print and who really does the work. The idea of technique dominates our interest, and discussions of prints often bog down in discussion of technique. We want to know how something is done, but we also want to know how well it is done, and there is a feeling that has lingered on in printing a little more than it has in painting that the viewer can measure technique and what is acceptable in technique. I think that is actually not true; my experience with technique has been that the viewer cannot tell as much as he thinks he can. For example, we may deliberately use misregistration. It is hard to do in editions, but it can be done, and you get effects from misregistration that you can't get any other way. I'm not advocating that everyone make blurry prints, but I am pointing out that all things are available to technique; you use them as you go and they are not so easy to reconstruct or judge.

Finally, we are left with some questions. We ask, is there really a graphic quality that stands on its own, independent from painting? What are the real relationships between printing and painting? The question is, can the artist feel and act with the same confidence and freedom in printing that he has in painting, or must printing be less expansive, less pictorial, and more confined? And we can allow printing to extend beyond the limits of its conventions?

Gutenberg and the Computer:
Disparate de Miedo (The Folly of Fear)[1]

DANIEL BELL

We are here because we are people *of* the Book: some by descent, others by the grammar of assent. There are those—sometimes they are even publishers—who are *in* the book (trade) but not of it. And there are those, to complete the logic of the metaphor, who are neither *in* nor *of* the Book.

Why defend the book? If it were only for antiquarian or sentimental reasons, there would be little rationale for the effort. We do so because the book—yes, as a format—is constitutive of culture. And without culture we live only the animal, the ignorant, or the utilitarian life.

As a sociologist, I begin with distinctions and categories in order to see what is at stake. There are five aspects of the book—I am being arbitrary, yet I hope to justify the number—that concern us today:

The first is the book as a utilitarian device, a means of organizing information in a convenient way.

The second is the book as a mode of learning, of gaining knowledge. Note that I distinguish between information and knowledge. This is a theme I shall return to as one of the axes of my argument.

The third is the book as text for entertainment, pleasure, and imagi-

---

1. The reference is, of course, to Goya's *Los Proverbios*, on the different follies of mankind. I recall with pleasure the brilliant, early impression of this print I saw at Lucien Goldschmidt's gallery. The image of this folly, to be didactic, is the thread of this talk.

nation. Here the focus is on language: the sounds and colors of language (as Mallarmé put it); the rhythms and sinuosity of language; the tropes and figurative modes that, by juxtaposition of terms, prompt the imagination to soar and to engage us actively as readers. The earliest words we may recall from childhood are: tell me a story; read me a book.

The fourth is the book as an aesthetic object itself, the pleasures of craft: the type, the layout of the page, the illustrations, the binding, all of which exemplify the art of the designer and the care of the craftsman.

And the fifth is the book as a 'collectible,' satisfying the hoarding impulse, the status desire, or the simple childish urge to collect objects that are 'mine.'

Some of these follies and fears can be quickly disposed of. In an air travel magazine—where else?—I read recently some advice about the extraordinary financial gains to be realized by collecting books. The head of a firm of book appraisers is quoted as advising the novice:

> . . . if you want a little fun, collect first editions of modern authors who you think will be recognized by posterity. Try to get the books signed by the author, a possibility not so remote now that publicity tours are arranged by publishers. An inscription or message increases the value.
>
> If, God forbid, you choose to read it, first remove the dust jacket; in part to keep that in good condition—it adds appreciably to the value of the book—and in part, because the shiny dust jacket takes up finger prints; the cloth jacket doesn't. Then put it away.

As a collectible, we can leave the book to the follies of the market.[2]

On the other hand, I think of a story about Gershom Scholem, the great authority on Jewish mysticism and himself a Master of the Book. Browsing one day in a bookstore in Jerusalem, Scholem found an extraordinary rare volume on the Lurianic kabbalah, a topic quite troublesome to many of the Orthodox. He asked the bookseller the price and was given an

---

2. The cognoscenti know, of course, that, as collectibles, first editions have now given way to the bound page galleys of advance reading copies, especially if they have authors' corrections photocopied on the pages, and are worth more, hallelujah, if *those* are signed by the author.

astonishingly low figure. Ashamed at the thought that he might be taking advantage of the man, Scholem said: 'Do you realize what this book is; how rare it is?' The bookseller looked at the book and shrugged: 'Some books are worth reading; some are not. The price is the same.' (It is only in secondhand bookstores that the principle of use-value, rather than exchange-value, sometimes applies.) We can leave rarity, subject to the follies of the market, modified, at times, by the good taste of the old-fashioned bookseller.

I leave aside, as well, the fate of the book as an aesthetic object: like prints, or good pottery, that will remain, an appreciation of design and taste in the history of craft and the arts.

My theme is the book in relation to information and knowledge, the fears about the book in the computer age and the questions of which fears may be justified and which are follies. And here, I have to step back in time to deal with the history, often forgotten, of some of these fears.

May I remind you (perhaps not necessary) that the book itself was not always sacrosanct, nor was writing? In the *Phaedo*, Plato states that writing was given to men to 'come to the rescue' of the 'weakness of discourse.' The gift of *grammata*—of the 'external' marks—was simply a crutch for memory. For Plato, knowledge is latent in our memories, the Ideas that are the true forms of reality. The drama is played out in the *Phaedrus*, the lovely dialogue about wisdom. The last part of the dialogue is about the inferiority of books and writing to thought and argument; of reading to reasoning; and of rhetoric to dialectic. Socrates is speaking. He tells of the king named Thamus, who dwelt in the city that the Greeks call Egyptian Thebes, while Thamus they call Ammon.

> To Ammon comes Theuth, who reveals some new arts to be given to the Egyptian people. One is writing. Theuth says: 'Here, O King, is a branch of learning that will make the people of Egypt wiser and improve their memories; my discovery provides a recipe for memory and wisdom.' To which the king answers that the effect of writing would be 'the very opposite of its true effect.'
>
> 'Their trust in writing, produced by external characters which

are not part of themselves, will discourage the use of their own memory within them. You have invented an elixir not of memory but of reminding; and you offer your pupils the appearance of wisdom, not true wisdom, for they will read many things without instruction and will therefore seem to know many things when they are for the most part ignorant. . . .' [Paragraphs 274 d, and 275]

The path to truth, as Plato puts it in the vivid metaphor in *The Republic*, is to cross 'the divided line,' to go from the visible to the intelligible, from opinion to knowledge. Yet beyond that, where even reading and writing cannot take us, is wisdom. As Socrates remarks in the *Phaedrus*:

> . . . one who has nothing to show of more value than the literary works on whose phrases he spends hours, twisting them this way and that, pasting them together and pulling them apart, will rightly, I suggest, be called a poet or speech writer or law writer. [Paragraph 278 e]

Those, however, who have done their work 'with a knowledge of truth'—here Socrates refers to Homer; to Lysias, a composer of discourses; and to Solon—are called lovers of wisdom. To call them wise would be going too far: 'the epithet is proper only to a god.'[3]

For Plato, writing—artificial aid, a device used by the sophists—is an anathema, a desecration of memory. But memory lives only through a collective community, tied together by culture. When the barbarians scatter the learned, ignorance rules, memory becomes untrustworthy and even a corrupter of texts and traditions. In the Middle Ages, the monasteries became the precious sources of conservation and transmission through the transcribing of texts. Gradually, invaluable libraries of classical and contemporary texts were created and new skills were established. Among the professional copyists, those who understood Greek took the highest place, and they bore the title of *scrittori*; the rest were simply called *copisti*. The

---

3. The translations above, other than paragraph 275, are from the Bollingen edition of the *Collected Dialogues*. For paragraph 275, I have used the Fowler/Loeb translation as being fuller and more explicit. For a more general discussion of the relation of memory to discourse, see Frances A. Yates, *The Art of Memory* (London: Routledge & Kegan Paul, 1966).

great library at Urbino, which Jacob Burckhardt describes in his *Civilization of the Renaissance in Italy*, employed thirty to forty *scrittori* and contained, in addition to classical texts, the complete Thomas Aquinas, a complete Albertus Magnus, and all of Dante and Boccaccio.

The book, now, with its beautiful script and illuminated initials, was not just a depository of learning but a work of art and admired as such. The invention of printing and the use of woodcuts for the illustration of books filled the duke of Urbino, the famous Federigo da Montefeltro, with such dismay that he would not allow a printed book to enter his library. For him, the act of reading a classical text was desecrated by the contemplation of the printed page. Words that were beautifully written by a scribe seemed to address his eye and mind in a personal way that was obliterated by mechanical type, and a manuscript illuminated by hand-painted miniatures gave him a pleasure that no woodcut could equal.

As Edgar Wind (whose description of the duke's reaction I have followed) points out, some of this may have been snobbery. Yet there were also good reasons, in the character of the first books, for his reaction:

> The first printed books were made to look like manuscripts, some were even doctored with hand-painted initials, or colored washes imposed on the woodcuts, or by being printed especially on vellum to satisfy the kind of fastidious taste which the Duke of Urbino had cultivated. Thus he cannot be entirely blamed for having regarded this new manufacture as an impertinent and vulgar cheat.[4]

---

4. Edgar Wind, *Art and Anarchy* (London: Faber & Faber, 1963). There was also resistance, of course, from the skilled craftsmen themselves. As Professor Teufelsdröckh from Weissnichtwo (who wanted to re-dress the world) declared in Carlyle's *Sartor Resartus*: 'He who first shortened the labor of Copyists by device of *Movable Type* was disbanding hired Armies and cashiering most Kings and Senates, and creating a whole new Democratic world; he had invented the art of Printing' (p. 40).

But that resistance was actually quite intense. As Warren Chappell points out, in his *Short History of the Printed Word* (New York: Alfred Knopf, 1970), p. 57:

> It seems incredible that the artifacts (the hand-press and bed) that led to the appearance of that first spectacular book to come from a press—Gutenberg's 42-line Bible—could have disappeared so completely. But it must be remembered that the scribes and illuminators wielded sufficient political power to have duplication of their work interdicted, except when done by hand.

DANIEL BELL

When a book is regarded as a work of art, rather than a utilitarian
format, the tension between craft and mechanization becomes an aesthetic
issue. When Ruskin spoke of 'vile manufacture' he contrasted all manufacture to honorable craftsmanship, in which the artist controlled his work
by his own hand, whereas in manufacture the production is surrendered
to an automation that mimics and therefore falsifies the work of the hand.[5]

Against this, one can, of course, counterpose the cult of the machine
as put forth by the Bauhaus, from Gropius to Moholy-Nagy, with its emphasis on the functional and machined quality of products in which ele-
gance is defined by the sheen of the metal or by the austere geometric line.

I do not mean to rehearse here the recurrent battle of the ancients and
the moderns, but reminiscence does lead me to speak, even if it is a mo-
mentary distraction, in praise of 'vile manufacture.'

When I was much younger, I used to work, as many of you may have,
in that great reference room of the New York Public Library, Room 315,
with its long tiers of tables, green shades, and the young pages who, paid
fifty cents an hour (a Depression work project), brought to one's table the
books one had ordered from the stacks. Those were the handicraft days of
research: writing out in long hand what other persons had written down
in books.

Much as I appreciated the treasures, I resented the place: I could not
smoke or drink coffee. I envied the presence of the long rows of reference
books along the walls. The image of the civilized life I envied most was a

---

5. It was only as recently as 1927—I say recently because it is within my lifetime—
that a great book designer could admit modern printing methods into the canon of 'the
book.' As Stanley Morison wrote about the Nonesuch Press:

> By making conscientious, and not merely commercial, use of modern methods, Mr.
> Meynell has gone far towards proving to many of us that the future of fine printing
> lies in the hands of those who are prepared to follow his lead and to use modern
> machinery. . . . Until the advent of the Nonesuch Press, mechanical composition
> was almost entirely identified with shoddy commercialism. Its use by one of the
> ablest modern typographers has, as we have said, resulted in the production of very
> fine works of art at a low price, and in the extension of interest in typography to a
> much wider public than could afford the works of the Victorian private presses.

Stanley Morison: *A Review of Recent Typography* (London: The Office of the Fleuron), re-
printed in the *Nonesuch Prospectus*, 1927, p. 20.

legend I had heard—a legend that Oscar Handlin later assured me was true—of a Harvard gentleman-scholar named Albert Bushnell Hart, who always purchased three copies of any book he wanted or needed. Why three? Mr. Hart (the Harvard snobbery is that professors call themselves Mister) never liked the handicraft of research. Since he did not wish to copy out any material, he bought one copy of a book for his shelves, and two for research. Why two? In the event that the material he needed to paste up continued on the other side of the page, of course.

Many years later, the son of a colleague, then awakening to the pleasures of books and scholarship, came into our apartment, looked at our library, and exclaimed: 'How come you have so many high-class paperbacks in hard cover, and two later copies in paperback besides?'

Let me turn to the present, as a prelude to looking ahead to the future. We are now on the rising slope of a third technological revolution, one that may transform our lives—in the processing of data, in the retrieval of information, in the organization of knowledge—in ways far beyond the first two technological revolutions of the past two hundred or so years.

Any numbering is to some extent arbitrary, and the word 'revolution,' with the implication of a sudden and abrupt change, is even more so. Yet we are subject also to convention, and, given the enormity of the changes we have seen, we can accept the term as meaningful. The first technological revolution, little more than two hundred years ago, was the introduction of compressed steam as a new form of energy. Commonplace as it now seems, we forget the extraordinary meaning of this simple idea of using the expansion of heated air from boiling water within a contained chamber to drive gears and shafts with great power. One has to go back to Leonardo da Vinci to grasp the significance of this change.

Leonardo, as you know, was not only a painter but an engineer and inventor whose restless imagination soared as few human beings' have done. In his notebooks, which we now have, he imagined an airplane, a submarine, refrigeration, a threshing machine—items that Francis Bacon delineated as the great achievements of Salomon's House, the research institute of science in his *New Atlantis*. Leonardo could imagine all these devices, and draw the machines that would drive them, with matchless precision and beauty, but he could not imagine one thing: a source of energy powerful enough to keep them moving steadily at sufficient speeds. The only sources of power he could think of were human muscle power, draft animal power, or natural wind or water power, and these were insufficient. James Watt's little 'tea kettle,' to use the metaphor of the fable, achieved that quantum jump in the application of energy to transform our worlds. And it did so in ways one scarcely thinks of. England is an island that is bedded on coal, but to go deep into the mines, one must pump out the water. Hand-operated pumps could do little. The introduction of steam pumps created the basis for the industrial revolution of England. And with steam, we have factories, railroads, steamships, and the like.

The second technological revolution, arbitrarily dated about a hundred years ago, was the introduction of electricity and chemistry. With electricity, we can code signals and send these along telegraph or telephone lines. We have a steady source of light, capable of being transmitted across long distances through electricity grids, which transforms our sense of night and day. And with electricity, we have a concentrated form of power that can send elevators hundreds of stories into the skies and propel engines at great speeds. Chemistry not only reorganizes the products of nature but, for the first time, creates man-made products, synthetics that had never before existed. With chemistry, we no longer think of things but of the 'properties' of things and the reorganization of properties to achieve (as with plastics) different purposes with our products.

And, now, the third technological revolution. We tend to think of technology in terms of 'things' and of the impact of 'things'—in this instance, the computer, telecommunications, and television. But this is to miss the way that technology now works its effects, and to fail to see an even more pervasive change in the relation of technology to science: the new centrality of the codification of theoretical knowledge.

The new technologies are embedded in a set of matrices, and one has to understand these in order to begin to explore the ramifications of the changes ahead.

The first is the fact that all our operating systems have moved from being electro-mechanical to purely electronic. A dial telephone is an electro-mechanical system in which an electric impulse 'pushes' a mechanical bar. An electronic system does its work entirely by electric impulse, thus eliminating the heavier and slower mechanical systems and replacing them with systems that are simpler and more reliable. What this does, more abstractly, is to replace all 'physical' systems. Think of the most pervasive 'pre-industrial' system of communication we have, the postal system. We still, in most instances, write a letter, place it in an envelope, affix a stamp, and drop it into a mailbox, where the letter is collected by a postman, taken to a local station, sorted, brought by truck to a depot, flown to another city, distributed to a local sub-station, sorted again for the specific locale, and brought by a postman to office or home by sack. Yet, over time, all this will be replaced, as has already happened within corporations transmitting documents from one office to another, by facsimile, an electronic system using telephone or cable lines. In all areas, from typewriters to television sets, the components become purely electronic.

The second matrix is even more 'conceptual.' It is the idea of *miniaturization*, the ability to 'shrink' components to microscopic sizes and to place hundreds of thousands of bytes of memory on a silicon chip the size of one's thumbnail. With miniaturization, we have 'command-and-control' units that can transmit millions of computations in fractions of a second and regulate liquid flows as in automobile motors, direct milling operations, and numerical-control machine tools. Miniaturization makes possible the personal computer and gives each individual the power that, a decade ago, could only be obtained in a room-sized machine.

The third matrix is *digitalization*, the conversion of transmission systems to pulsed operations. The telephone, historically, has been an analogue system, in which sound proceeds like a wave. Some early computers were analogue computers, in which speeds and measurements 'matched' other measures, such as the minute hand of a clock or watch, or the height of the mercury in a thermometer. Digital systems are 'discrete' and expressed in numbers, as in digital watches or the binary codes of computer switches. Since computers now work almost entirely on a digital basis, the conversion of all other systems, such as the telephone or television systems, to digital modes, through switching devices, makes them all compatible with one another and allows for cross-switching and interchange of use, as in railroad switching systems that can mix all kinds of cars on their tracks.

Yet behind all this, as I indicated earlier, is something more important and pervasive: the meshing of technology with science and the directive role of theoretical knowledge. Every society we know has been based on knowledge, and what distinguishes us from animal societies is our ability to codify sounds into speech, speech into alphanumeric symbols, and the symbols into written texts for transmission beyond the life of any generation. But it is only in this century that the codification of theoretical knowledge has become central for directing innovation. Let me take three illustrations.

The computer, as we know it, would have been impossible within the conceptions of classical physics. Only with the revolutions that created quantum mechanics did we get a new conception of solid-state matter and the structure of subatomic particles. Niels Bohr gave us the first model of the atom (ca. 1913), which allowed us to plot the movement of electrons in orbit. A decade and a half later, Felix Bloch (who spent his émigré years fruitfully at Stanford) provided the picture of the lattice structure of the atom, which showed how the electrons jumped from orbit to orbit. And in 1940, at Bell Labs, Bardeen, Brittain, and Shockley invented the transistor, which opened up the entire field of semiconductors and provided the route to miniaturization. The trace-lines are distinct.

In 1905, at the age of twenty-eight, Albert Einstein wrote three papers for the *Annalen der Physik*, any one of which would have won him lasting fame in the history of science. One was on the Brownian motion, which 'proved' the existence of atoms. The second was on special relativity, which revised Newton's concept of absolute rest and the fixed coordinates of space and time to establish the speed of light as the 'ultimate' constant and to put space and time onto a single continuum. And the third, which had the most immediate impact—and for which Einstein won the Nobel prize in 1919—demonstrated that light was a quantum, which was discontinuous, rather than only a wave. This paper, popularly called the 'photo-electric effect,' led to such 'simple' devices as the broken light beam, which opens and closes elevator doors, and the laser (light amplified by stimulated emission of radiation), developed by Charles Townes at Columbia in the 1950s. What Einstein did, simply, was to revolutionize the field of optics.

And in the development of the computer, theory preceded practice. Though the physical idea of the computer was envisaged long ago in the abacus, and Charles Babbage, the Cambridge mathematician, had in the 1830s sketched the way a calculating machine could operate, the fundamental logic of the computer was laid out in a theoretical paper, 'On Computable Numbers,' by another Cambridge mathematician (and logician), Alan M. Turing, in 1936. In that paper, Turing set out the nature and theoretical structure of logic machines, as mechanisms of decisions, before there was any symbolic description or physical embodiment of that logic in an electronic device. Yet Turing's paper provided the logical foundations of all 'decision' machines.

Nineteenth-century invention was largely a matter of trial-and-error by talented tinkerers, such as an Edison or a Marconi, quite independent of (and often indifferent to) the work in theoretical knowledge. What is decisive for innovation, and for all intellectual disciplines today, is the primacy of theoretical knowledge. It is a theorem that is fundamental to the understanding of our age, and it is the failure to understand this crucial point that has led, as I shall try to show, to the blurring of the distinctions between data, information, and knowledge and to the pervasive yet blowzy images of 'the information age' and other misleading tags about our time.

We begin, now, to approach the heart of the matter. What is—will be, may be—the effect of the computer, or electronic publishing—or the third technological revolution—on 'the Book'?

The book, in many ways, is a pre-industrial, artisan, handicraft kind of item even though an individual best seller may sell a million or more copies. The industry produces forty thousand or so different trade books a year, plus textbooks, specialized scholarly books, technical and scientific monographs, reference books, religious tracts, hobby and game books, and so on. Books are sold through mail, through old-fashioned bookstores, through chain-owned flashy bookstores, through supermarkets, through college textbook stores, through religious bookshops, and the like. Perhaps the commodity that most approximates the book is the shoe. There are men's shoes and women's shoes and children's shoes, all in diverse sizes. They are of leather, rubber, suede, nylon, and other materials. There are boots and espadrilles, stylish and expensive designer shoes, and simple, mass-produced sneakers and sandals. A store has to carry a large inventory, and each customer must be fitted separately for size, taste, and purpose.

Why do I make this outlandish comparison? Because some people assume that the future of the book may be like the future of the shoe, if the idea of 'auto-shoe' ever becomes feasible. 'Auto-shoe' is the vision of Michael Dertouzos, who directs the Laboratory of Computer Science at M.I.T. For him, the prototype of auto-shoe, as he has envisaged it and even designed it, may be the way that shoes, and similar commodities, may be produced in the future.[6] In this glossy new world, a patron enters an auto-shoe shop. On one wall are different banks of images. The top bank carries images of different materials: leather, vinyl, suede, and so on. A second bank has different colors along the spectrum, pure or in combination. A third bank illustrates different styles: open toe, buck, monk's strap, wingtip, and others. The patron places his or her feet on a metal plate, and a holographic image sketches the exact contour of the foot in three dimensions. From a console at the side, the patron now begins to press buttons for the different combinations of materials, colors, and style that he or she desires. And, as images, they are flashed onto the foot. When finally satisfied, he or she enters the console numbers on a tape, pulls a lever, and within X minutes a bespoke shoe, to the exact fit and taste, is delivered to the customer. One does not have to have a huge inventory of different styles and sizes. Nor does one need a clerk, rushing back and forth and bending over to try and satisfy the whims of the customer. Auto-shoe becomes the simple, automated production system to turn production away from the costly, mass-produced system of countless items to the customized needs and taste of the buyer.

6. In *The Computer Age*, edited by Michael M. Dertouzos and Joel Moses (Cambridge: M.I.T. Press, 1979).

And why not 'auto-book'? The different technologies are all there—in principle. One can have on-demand publishing, in which an order is placed through a computer network and the 'book' is sent as a burst of print by wire to a desk-top copier. Presumably a four-hundred-page book could be sent in four minutes—at a cost. More realistically, one can get 'books' on floppy disks, to be inserted into a computer, or a 'book' could be 'etched' on a laser card or chip, and a page projected on an LED screen. Of course, encyclopedias can be stored in information-retrieval systems, and particular articles or sections of information recalled onto a screen.

On the production side, authors can (and some now do) deliver copy in machine-readable form on magnetic tape or disks, or provide camera-ready copy, coded for appropriate typeface and book design, which can go into a computerized production system. (It is recorded that Mark Twain was the first author to submit a typewritten manuscript for book production. It is not known who may claim that 'first' distinction for machine-readable tapes.)

This combination of computerized production and computerized re-call and ordering is the basis of electronic publishing, in which, through different vendors, 'information' is available to individuals with receivers—either personal computers or, in the case of some Videotex system, through the television sets in one's home. Twenty or so years ago, relatively clear boundaries separated computer services (data processing), broadcast com-munications (radio, television), telephone services, and publishing. The technologies involved in each line were distinct, and few companies over-lapped. Today there are crossings and switchings, and one finds oneself intertwined in a variety of different technologies and services. One of my colleagues, Paul Starr, has studied this problem and has observed that 'Publishing has now become so enmeshed with computers and data-base services that some say publishers should stop thinking of themselves as producers of books or periodicals and recognize that they are information suppliers, not bound to any particular medium.'

It would seem that the technologies of photocopying and information-retrieval have made all that anachronistic. But is that really so?

A book is a format—the placing of words, using a standardized type, with ink, on paper. What difference does it make if one reads what one needs on a screen or on a printout, rather than within the pages of a bound book? These are the questions that engage the industry. But I want to shift the discussion from production and marketing and distribution to more relevant intellectual issues and the follies and fears that have been exaggerated or obscured.

The first question is: what are we talking about? In a letter to John Cole, the director of a Library of Congress study on the future of the book, an advisory-committee member writes:

> I am enormously fond of books. . . . Nevertheless I am not convinced that they are the most effective means of communicating information that can be developed. We are living in an age of exploding knowledge. There is so much to know.

But this is all wrong, for the writer is confusing *information* with *knowledge*, and the two are not the same. Information is news, facts, statistics, reports, legislation, tax codes, judicial decisions, resolutions, and the like, and it is quite obvious that we have had an 'explosion' of these not only with the multiplication of organizations but because all countries (and the wars between them), and the diverse world polities (and their factions), and the worldwide economy now come under our daily scrutiny in newspapers and television and in the pages of specialized magazines. But that is not necessarily (or even usually) knowledge. Knowledge is interpretation in context, exegesis, relatedness, and conceptualization, the forms of argument. The results of knowledge are theories: the effort to establish relevant relationships or connections between facts, data, and other information in some coherent form and to explain the reasons for those generalizations.

Perhaps the simplest way of suggesting (not defining) these distinctions is to think of an index at the end of a book. The *name index* is like data; it is simply the listing of the proper names of the individuals (or countries or places) that are mentioned in the book. The *subject index* is information; it is the statement of categories under which topics and names are placed. The *analytical index* (which few authors any longer bother with, but which any serious reader of a book will construct himself) is like knowledge; it is the establishment of relations and cross-references, based on intellectual purposes, in order to understand the logic of argument or the nature of the phenomena being analyzed. And we know how difficult that is.

The computer is a marvelous tool for scholars, when it is used for the purposes of information. At Harvard, the Classics Department owns an Anglo-Saxon concordance, an index of all the words in Old English showing the different places where any word occurred. The concordance is the equivalent of ten thousand pages of text, but placed on a PDP 11/44, it fits neatly onto a disk the size of a phonograph record. If you wish to find a reference to a kitchen, or to food, or to fishing, or any activity of the kind, you can locate every example of phrases where these words appear. The University of California at Irvine has been constructing a Thesaurus Linguae Graecae—a data bank that will include sixty-five million words of ancient Greek literature. A professor preparing, say, a paper on family pets in the ancient world could request every single use of 'dog' or 'cat' (though he would have to know which animals were used as pets; imagine a scholar a hundred years hence seeking to understand American culture and finding the word 'lynx' associated with the planet Mercury) and could even write a scholarly paper on the use of the word *dog* in Homer, Plato, Aristotle, and the Cynics (but could he distinguish between a philosopher and a dog?).

The intellectual issue arises when one asks: what are you looking for, and why? Some judgment has to be made initially, and that judgment has to be related to some intellectual or utilitarian purpose, otherwise one is simply computerizing Borges's Library of Babel, in which every word ever uttered has its place in the 'data bank' of the endless stacks, or disks, of utterances. An interesting model of a computerized search is the system called Lexis (operated by the Mead Corporation), used in legal research. All the decisions of judges in different courts around the country are entered into the system and updated continually. It contains a system of key words, and a legal researcher seeking to find precedents or rules applicable to his own problem uses the key words to retrieve decisions, and paragraphs of decisions, that seem relevant to what he needs. By interacting with the system, he can rove to and fro, as if turning the pages of a book, but guided by the key words, like Ariadne's thread, to the different or conflicting views on the problem relevant to him. But Lexis is relatively successful because it has a bounded universe, explicit rules to relate key words, and an obvious pay-off in the retrieved precedents or rules to justify the costs of maintaining the system. A bounded universe such as Old English or the ancient Greek world may justify similar efforts. But all that is largely on the level of information. If one wishes to relate material from one culture to another, then a very different process of search and judgment ensues and—unless every book, document, marriage register, land roll, contract, and literary work were computerized—the process is costly and, in the end, meaningless.

Another way of looking at the question is to ask: *how* do we read? One can skim, or 'mine,' a text (by Hi-lighter or pencil), or 'talk' to the text (Augustine recalls in surprise that when he ventured onto Ambrose in his study, Ambrose was reading *silently*; a wholly novel mode at the time), or reflect and re-phrase a text. It is in this context that we can begin to assess the role of the computer and the newer modes of electronic, electrostatic, or optical reproduction.

If one's purposes are *information*, clearly defined, then the book is obsolete. The storage in a computer or optical (laser disk) memory, the rapidity of access, the ability to revise—all this makes the newer modes preferable to a book. If one is a researcher—a sociologist or a physician or an engineer—one can take a community fact-book, opinion-survey data, market research, census material, health data, and judicial decisions and 'update' these readily and, with computer graphics, convert the digitalized data readily into graphs or bar charts or some other pictorial mode. Those findings can then be 'manipulated' to re-analyze the previous data in the light of the new material, thus establishing time-series or time-frames that provide a deeper awareness of the nature of these materials or finds.

But if one reads to reflect, to 'talk' to the work, to construct an argument, or to interpret a passage, then it is more likely that the format of the book, with its margins and convenience, may be a better mode. Or, as Dr. Jerome Lettvin (who is professor of communications, physiology, and bioengineering in the Departments of Computer Science, Biology, and Electrical Engineering at M.I.T.) writes:

. . . if I had an electronic library at my command, like the Library of Congress, where I could type in an instruction and it would let me look at such and such a book that would lead to another related book or article, and so forth—that could be of use to me only occasionally. Of much more use would be a library where, when I'm looking for one book I may find another next to it on the shelf that I am really much more interested in. . . .

This is the notion of ambient context that is extremely rich in information value, but is very vaguely defined. But now with current computer architecture, that ambient context gets pushed out of the system. In other words, you are supposed to be like the machines that you operate: specifically goal-oriented by a specific logic, and in a particular way, you can see perfectly clearly what data you are going to have.

Leafing through a book is very different from having a screen run very rapidly past you. I am an old believer in the notion that perception is an active and not a passive thing. That is, you move your eyes to perceive; you move your hands to proceed; you know you move to look. I do not want to have the aspect of everything that I would want to touch brought to me. . . .

The author of a book called *Turing's Man*, comparing the scholar with a pen and the scientist and philosopher at a computer terminal, writes: 'The scientist or philosopher who works with such electronic tools will think in different ways from those who have worked at ordinary desks with paper and pencil.'

But will this be so? What is being claimed in such elaborate hyperbole is a new definition of man: not as *homo faber*, the tool-user, or *homo pictor*, the symbol-using animal, but man as 'information processor,' in which Mind is mapped through codes and algorithms. Methodology in the seventeenth century, as defined by Descartes, denoted the discipline that would establish a universal method (mathematics) that would answer any question in a compatible-scientific way. And Leibniz dreamt of a machine that, if one programmed a question, would immediately flash the answer. A century later, De la Mettrie claimed that *man* is a machine (though he died of gout, probably from stoking the machine too much). Now we have the vision of man as artificial intelligence, a programmable reed. This is the heart of the matter, or the heart of darkness.

Behind all this is a fundamental epistemological issue that has roiled philosophy in recent years—the effort in the twentieth century, particularly of Frege, Russell, and Carnap, to establish unambiguous meanings through the use of constructed languages. Let me simply say that after Quine and the later Wittgenstein, it is difficult to sustain the argument that words *represent* things, that there is a 'correspondence theory' of truth. This may be somewhat true of information. We may even have pictorial dictionaries, such as Japanese-English, to point to pictured things and give us the word in each language, yet there has to be some common context of understanding; otherwise, a piece of glass in a frame may 'mean' a television set to a Western person but only a poor mirror to the !Kung bushmen.

Words, in the context of knowledge—for judgment, evaluation, interpretation—are clues to behavior or guides to action; meanings are grasped in usage; terms are embedded in culture; actions are regulated by rules that derive from agreement. We 'construct' reality through the different prisms we employ.

The computer modes are computational and sequential. Everything is played out according to the rules of a formal system, and these rules are finite (otherwise, the computer would go on clacking into infinity). And one seeks an algorithm or decision rule that tells the best way of solving a problem.[7]

---

7. Turing's 1936 paper, it should be pointed out, had a double edge. On the one hand it sought to answer Hilbert's 'third question.' In 1928, the great German mathematician David Hilbert, in his effort to formalize all mathematics, had asked three questions: could mathematics be *complete*, so that every statement could either be proved or disproved; could it be shown to be *consistent* in that the valid steps of proof could not be used for false conclusions; and was mathematics *decidable*; namely, was there a definite method that would, in principle, be applied to any assertion and produce a correct decision on the truth or falsity of that assertion.

Soon after, the young Czech mathematician Kurt Gödel demonstrated that the first two propositions were unprovable, even if true, thus shattering the hopes for a complete

Surely one cannot quarrel with these possibilities, so long as one can clearly define a problem, establish the parameters, spell out the alternative combinations and permutations, and trace out the 'one best way,' or optimal solution. This was the dream of Pascal and the vision of a Laplacean universe. If the world is a 'logical set,' then reduction of thought to computational modes is a possible goal. But the problem is not just 'the world' (and the question whether there is a constitutive order to its internal connections), but the language we use, imperfectly, to describe and understand the world—of nature, society, and the self.

There is, first, the question of *formalization*. Natural language is created and re-worked by usage, and the effort to establish underlying rules —say, of homologies—so that we can have an algorithm that will classify sentences correctly runs afoul of the messiness of natural language. An adept of Fowler will immediately understand why. Take the problem of *syllepsis* and *zeugma*, two figures of speech often confused with one another:

---

formalization of mathematics. Turing took on the third question. He constructed a 'machine' that could 'read' any 'table of behavior' of a finite set and compute all the possible combinations of answers to derivations from the original number. These were 'computable numbers,' any real number (i.e., the rational and irrational numbers, such as $\sqrt{2}$ whose decimal places continue in an unending and non-repeating sequence) that was defined by some definite set of rules. The 'machine' could arrive at every number generated through arithmetical operations, every number that could arise in computational mathematics. But Turing's 'machine' also demonstrated a limit. An uncomputable number would be an example of an unsolvable problem, so there could not be a definite method for solving all mathematical questions. Thus, the answer to Hilbert's third question was 'no.'

On the other hand, Turing had found a 'mechanical means,' i.e., outside human intervention, to solve in principle any computational problem arrived at within mathematics. As his biographer, Andrew Hodges, writes: '[Turing] had proved that there was no "miraculous machine" that could solve all mathematical problems, but in the process he had discovered something almost equally miraculous, the idea of a universal machine that could take over the work of *any* machine.'

For a precise discussion of Turing's work, see Andrew Hodges, *Alan Turing: The Enigma* (New York: Simon & Schuster, 1983), especially pp. 91–110. This book should not be confused with *Turing's Man: Western Culture in the Computer Age*, by J. David Bolter (Chapel Hill: The University of North Carolina Press, 1984), a shallow work that makes extravagant claims for the consequences of the computer on modes of thought.

Syllepsis: Miss Bolo went home in a flood of tears and a sedan chair.
(Or)
He lost his hat and temper.
Zeugma: With weeping eyes and hearts (Or)
Kill the boys and the luggage. (From Shakespeare's
Henry V)

The syllepsis is grammatically correct (even though outlandish) but requires a single word to be understood *in a different sense with each of its pair*. In the zeugma, the single word fails to give sense with one of its pair, so that for the meaning to be clear an additional word is needed, such as 'Kill the boys and *destroy* the luggage.'

At stake is the relation of syntax to semantics, of word order to meaning. In writing homologous rules, one requires a common syntax. Yet such an algorithm cannot deal with the nature of idiom. For example: a) She drove him to school. b) She drove him to drink. Syntactically, they are homologous; semantically, quite different.[8]

But the fundamental questions are not the technical complexities of grammar, formidable as they are, but the nature of thought and the 'reductionism' that the computational mode seeks to introduce. We can, in one instance, follow a distinction of John Dewey's (in his *Art as Experience*). Dewey admired science and thought its methods and modes of inquiry one of the great achievements of intelligence. Yet Dewey distinguished between *expression* and *statement*. Science states meanings; art expresses them. Statements set forth the conditions under which knowledge can be gained

---

8. I will leave aside the problem of an algorithm for the correct usages of the auxiliaries *shall* and *should*, *will* and *would*. Otto Jespersen took one hundred and seventeen pages in his *Modern English Grammar on Historical Principles* to explore the distinctions, recording seven hundred years of inconsistency and shifting usages. Fowler, in *The King's English*, devotes twenty-one pages to *shall* and *will* and, in despair, says: 'It is unfortunate that the idiomatic use, while it comes by nature to southern Englishmen . . . is so complicated that those who are not to the manner born can hardly acquire it.'

Since the terms involve the problems of conditional, volitional, and obligational (ought to), not to mention the quasi-conditional and quasi-volitional, the need for clarity and consistency is great, but whether, hopefully, that need can be met is a question not yet answered.

Hopefully? Hopefully! But we will not go into that thicket.

or an experience may be derived. Yet 'the poetic as distinct from prosaic, esthetic as distinct from science, expression as distinct from statement, does something different from leading to an experience. It *constitutes* one.' (Emphasis added.)

The poetic expression is thinking in tropes. One is not pointing to things but expanding the imagination through metaphor and metonomy, through allegory and parable. The converse is reification, the frozen mimicry of thought to which ideology reduces speech. The crown and the sceptre invoke a sense of history and the sweep of pageantry; the Kremlin and the White House, the dreary rhetoric of political cliché. Thinking by the pathways of the 'electronic tool' risks constriction of the blood vessels of thought; the book allows the mind to soar.

In another instance, we can turn to Kant, who brought metaphysics from the world and its predicates to Mind and its categories. For Kant, what we know is a function of the categories or concepts we establish: we perceive facts but we create relationships, selecting from the blooming buzzing confusion the aspects of the world we seek to understand. Yet behind it all, in the noumena that we cannot fathom, is what Kant called 'the mystery of synthesis.' How do we put together, and why, the different components of what we puzzle out from the world? Man's creative capacity begins with the pervasive prefix, *re*. What distinguishes us from other species is our ability to re-organize, re-arrange, re-order our experiences and to re-design our world. But the art and the act remain a mystery.

The world is double-storied: a logical order on a factual disorder. But there is no single logical order. Throughout a single day we experience, literally, millions of 'bits' of experience, hear of and read about thousands of events, meet and talk to hundreds of persons, yet in the end we select a small portion, what we judge to be 'relevant,' and group these together, in recall, as the knowledge worth remembering. It is theory that decides what we observe, wrote Einstein: 'There is no inductive method which could lead to the fundamental concepts of physics.' What complicates our understanding is that our picture of the world comes from a limited experiential basis, yet the laws of physics contradict our mundane movement in the world and derive from a leap that is not the leap of faith but the leap of imagination. The difficulty in grasping the idea of special relativity, and its denial of a Newtonian world (or more accurately, the restriction of a Newtonian world to a delimited range of relationships), comes from our view of universal time, applicable to all observers, and of events in space as a whole, ideas that derive from our everyday experience in observing the sequence of events. Yet the idea of the dilation of time, of no 'absolute' standard for the measurement of time, makes no sense in a world ordered by Chronos and his metrical wand. Deprived of any certainty that our concepts have a connection with corresponding experiences, as my colleague Gerald Holton puts it, we begin to see the precariousness of theory construction as well. Or as Einstein quite picturesquely put it (in his essay on the space-time continuum, in the older *Britannica*), citing a Talmudic parable: Who first discovered water? We do not know. But the fish did not.

How to stand 'outside ourselves,' to achieve the necessary intellectual and aesthetic distance that allows us to re-order and re-arrange our worlds, is an act of creativity that we still do not understand. That is where imagination and science (a simple definition of knowledge) join.

Erasmus dedicated his *Moriae Encomium*, *The Praise of Folly*, to Sir Thomas More, who earlier had met the fate of those who oppose capricious authority. 'Farewell eloquent More, and stoutly defend your Moriae,' wrote Erasmus. And, as he wrote in his *Praise*: 'There are two main obstacles to gaining knowledge of things: shame, which clouds the mind; and fear, which, once the danger has been sighted, urges one not to perform the action. From both of these, Folly grandly frees us.'